HAPPINESS IS A SERIES OF GOOD DECISIONS · LIVE DIRECTIONALLY · IT'S ONLY A PROBLEM · DO WHAT WORKS · TRADITIONS: HONOR THEM. CREATE THEM. KEEP THEM. · IF IT'S NOT RIGHT, GO LEFT · LOVE IS A CHOICE · STAY IN YOUR LANE · STOP WINE-ING · BEGIN. FOCUS. COMMIT. · CHANGE IS HARD AND CHANGE IS GOOD

EM · IF IT'S NOT RIGHT, GO LEFT · LOVE IS A CHOICE · STAY IN YOUR LANE · STOP WINE—
YOU MAKE IT A PROBLEM · BEGIN. FOCUS. COMMIT. · CHANGE IS HARD AND CHANGE IS
GHT, GO LEFT · LOVE IS A CHOICE · STAY IN YOUR LANE · STOP WINE—ING · HAPPINESS
PROBLEM · BEGIN. FOCUS. COMMIT. · CHANGE IS HARD AND CHANGE IS GOOD · DO WHAT
VE IS A CHOICE · STAY IN YOUR LANE · STOP WINE—ING · HAPPINESS IS A SERIES OF GOO
CUS. COMMIT. · CHANGE IS HARD AND CHANGE IS GOOD · DO WHAT WORKS · TRADITIONS
AY IN YOUR LANE · STOP WINE—ING · HAPPINESS IS A SERIES OF GOOD DECISIONS · LIVE
ANGE IS HARD AND CHANGE IS GOOD · DO WHAT WORKS · TRADITIONS: HONOR THEM. CRE
TOP WINE—ING · HAPPINESS IS A SERIES OF GOOD DECISIONS · LIVE DIRECTIONALLY · IT
ANGE IS GOOD · DO WHAT WORKS · TRADITIONS: HONOR THEM. CREATE THEM. KEEP THE
PPINESS IS A SERIES OF GOOD DECISIONS · LIVE DIRECTIONALLY · IT'S ONLY A PROBLEM
O WHAT WORKS · TRADITIONS: HONOR THEM. CREATE THEM. KEEP THEM · IF IT'S NOT RIG
GOOD DECISIONS · LIVE DIRECTIONALLY · IT'S ONLY A PROBLEM IF YOU MAKE IT A PR
ADITIONS: HONOR THEM. CREATE THEM. KEEP THEM · IF IT'S NOT RIGHT, GO LEFT · LOVE
IVE DIRECTIONALLY · IT'S ONLY A PROBLEM IF YOU MAKE IT A PROBLEM · BEGIN. FOCUS.
EATE THEM. KEEP THEM · IF IT'S NOT RIGHT, GO LEFT · LOVE IS A CHOICE · STAY IN YO
T'S ONLY A PROBLEM IF YOU MAKE IT A PROBLEM · BEGIN. FOCUS. COMMIT. · CHANGE IS
EM · IF IT'S NOT RIGHT, GO LEFT · LOVE IS A CHOICE · STAY IN YOUR LANE · STOP WINE—
YOU MAKE IT A PROBLEM · BEGIN. FOCUS. COMMIT. · CHANGE IS HARD AND CHANGE IS
GHT, GO LEFT · LOVE IS A CHOICE · STAY IN YOUR LANE · STOP WINE—ING · HAPPINESS
PROBLEM · BEGIN. FOCUS. COMMIT. · CHANGE IS HARD AND CHANGE IS GOOD · DO WHAT
VE IS A CHOICE · STAY IN YOUR LANE · STOP WINE—ING · HAPPINESS IS A SERIES OF GOO
CUS. COMMIT. · CHANGE IS HARD AND CHANGE IS GOOD · DO WHAT WORKS · TRADITIONS
AY IN YOUR LANE · STOP WINE—ING · HAPPINESS IS A SERIES OF GOOD DECISIONS · LIVE
ANGE IS HARD AND CHANGE IS GOOD · DO WHAT WORKS · TRADITIONS: HONOR THEM. CR
TOP WINE—ING · HAPPINESS IS A SERIES OF GOOD DECISIONS · LIVE DIRECTIONALLY · IT
ANGE IS GOOD · DO WHAT WORKS · TRADITIONS: HONOR THEM. CREATE THEM. KEEP TH
PPINESS IS A SERIES OF GOOD DECISIONS · LIVE DIRECTIONALLY · IT'S ONLY A PROBLE
O WHAT WORKS · TRADITIONS: HONOR THEM. CREATE THEM. KEEP THEM · IF IT'S NOT RIG
GOOD DECISIONS · LIVE DIRECTIONALLY · IT'S ONLY A PROBLEM IF YOU MAKE IT A PI
ADITIONS: HONOR THEM. CREATE THEM. KEEP THEM · IF IT'S NOT RIGHT, GO LEFT · LOVE
IVE DIRECTIONALLY · IT'S ONLY A PROBLEM IF YOU MAKE IT A PROBLEM · BEGIN. FOCUS.
EATE THEM. KEEP THEM · IF IT'S NOT RIGHT, GO LEFT · LOVE IS A CHOICE · STAY IN YO
T'S ONLY A PROBLEM IF YOU MAKE IT A PROBLEM · BEGIN. FOCUS. COMMIT. · CHANGE IS
EM · IF IT'S NOT RIGHT, GO LEFT · LOVE IS A CHOICE · STAY IN YOUR LANE · STOP WINE—
YOU MAKE IT A PROBLEM · BEGIN. FOCUS. COMMIT. · CHANGE IS HARD AND CHANGE IS
GHT, GO LEFT · LOVE IS A CHOICE · STAY IN YOUR LANE · STOP WINE—ING · HAPPINESS
PROBLEM · BEGIN. FOCUS. COMMIT. · CHANGE IS HARD AND CHANGE IS GOOD · DO WHAT
VE IS A CHOICE · STAY IN YOUR LANE · STOP WINE—ING · HAPPINESS IS A SERIES OF GOO
CUS. COMMIT. · CHANGE IS HARD AND CHANGE IS GOOD · DO WHAT WORKS · TRADITIONS
AY IN YOUR LANE · STOP WINE—ING · HAPPINESS IS A SERIES OF GOOD DECISIONS · LIVE
ANGE IS HARD AND CHANGE IS GOOD · DO WHAT WORKS · TRADITIONS: HONOR THEM. CR
STOP WINE—ING · HAPPINESS IS A SERIES OF GOOD DECISIONS · LIVE DIRECTIONALLY · IT
ANGE IS GOOD · DO WHAT WORKS · TRADITIONS: HONOR THEM. CREATE THEM. KEEP TH
PPINESS IS A SERIES OF GOOD DECISIONS · LIVE DIRECTIONALLY · IT'S ONLY A PROBLE
DO WHAT WORKS · TRADITIONS: HONOR THEM. CREATE THEM. KEEP THEM · IF IT'S NOT RIG
GOOD DECISIONS · LIVE DIRECTIONALLY · IT'S ONLY A PROBLEM IF YOU MAKE IT A P
ADITIONS: HONOR THEM. CREATE THEM. KEEP THEM · IF IT'S NOT RIGHT, GO LEFT · LOVE
IVE DIRECTIONALLY · IT'S ONLY A PROBLEM IF YOU MAKE IT A PROBLEM · BEGIN. FOCUS

IF IT'S NOT RIGHT,

GO LEFT

IF IT'S NOT RIGHT,
GO LEFT

*Practical and Inspirational
Lessons to Move You in
a Positive Direction*

KRISTEN GLOSSERMAN

ISBN: 978-1-951412-17-3
Ebook ISBN: 978-1-951412-44-9
LCCN: 2020915634

Photo credits:
By Liza Gershman: pages 2, 24, 26, 32, 38, 46, 52, 62, 68, 75, 80, 83, 86, 89,
108, 112, 135, 138, 140, 149, 158, 164, 167, 170, 175
By Madison Fender, copyright © 2021: pages 6, 37, 41, 55, 72, 76, 105, 107,
119, 120, 128, 131, 151, 152, 162
From Del Vecchio family photo collection: page 176

Manufactured in China.

Design by David Miles

10 9 8 7 6 5 4 3 2 1

The Collective Book Studio
Oakland, California
www.thecollectivebook.studio

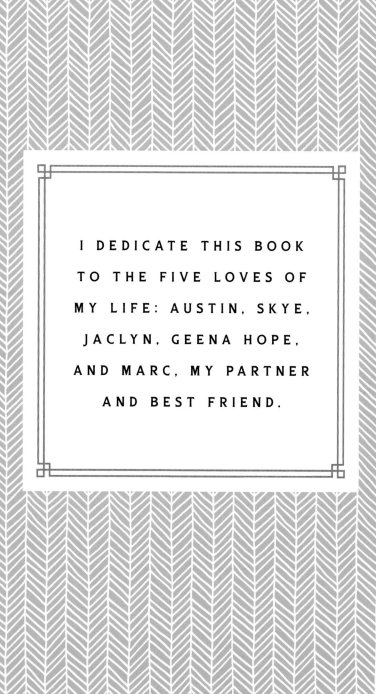

I DEDICATE THIS BOOK
TO THE FIVE LOVES OF
MY LIFE: AUSTIN, SKYE,
JACLYN, GEENA HOPE,
AND MARC, MY PARTNER
AND BEST FRIEND.

CONTENTS

INTRODUCTION

THE PAGES AHEAD CONTAIN A COMBINATION OF MY story and my coaching philosophy: a thirty-year-plus journey to move myself toward a more positive life, and a set of Life Lessons—teachings, observations, and suggestions—I've organized to help you undertake a similar journey.

The eleven Life Lessons I distilled for the book began to take shape at a moment in my life when I suddenly found myself in a place of tragedy and emotional hardship. The lessons have evolved ever since, and I continue to use them every day to help me find my direction, and every day these practices makes me a better, happier person. The lessons keep me grounded and always moving forward—I think of them as an eleven-part program, my own personal self-help manual, and I'm so happy to offer these pages to you.

These lessons have been so important in my daily life that it didn't occur to me at first how much more I would rely on them while living through the frightening COVID-19 pandemic of 2020 and its stressful quarantine days—in fact, I wrote this book throughout the crisis, and that gave me a renewed and heightened sense of how the lessons I was defining give me strength and guidance on ordinary days, on great days, and especially in times of uncertainty.

My point is this: Whether we like it or not, life happens, and it's up to us to decide how we respond. I believe in embracing change. Change can be motivating and inspiring if you allow it to be, so the first thing I will ask is for you to embrace change as well, because we just never know what life will throw at us.

As we move through the flow of our days, there will always be things that challenge us—some big, some small, often unexpected obstacles we need to move through and grow from. Don't allow these tough times to overwhelm you. Try to find the good in each day, and let that be your motivator and your strength. These lessons will help you do that.

Again, it's not going to be an easy journey, committing to a program of new ways of perceiving and new kinds of actions. Just hang in there and keep moving forward in the direction of the positive. You will not be sorry you did.

I believe that the lessons in this book have saved me, time and time again, from negative paths and less-than-positive spirals. They are the reason I was able to become the person I am today—truly and deeply happy. My goal with this book is that the lessons within will be a powerful guide for you on your own journey, providing clarity, inspiration, and positivity as you find your path to a happy and fulfilling life.

Read on, and as I say in a rallying cheer for all the work I do with making connections and embracing change: Hope This Helps!

—Kristen

ON A VERY PERSONAL NOTE

I was just thirteen years old when tragedy struck our family: My brother, Michael, died in a skiing accident. That terrible day marked the beginning of the hardest time of my life. Michael passed away on December 30, while we were in Vermont for the winter holidays. My parents had us gather our things and get in the car, and we headed back to Long Island in the middle of the night, my mom's cousins following us in their car. I remember looking out the back window as we were leaving Vermont and realizing that my life and the lives of my parents, sister, Tara, and other relatives would never be the same.

We arrived home safely after a long and grueling drive that seemed endless and yet will forever be a blur to me. The next day, New Year's Eve, the holiday spirit in our home was displaced by the all-consuming loss of my brother. For decades afterward, the sound of Christmas music always sent me into a depression.

To get me out of the house, my best friend, Jennifa, and her mother, Annette, picked me up and took me out for Chinese food, along with Annette's two sisters. Annette's family saved me that night. They surrounded me with love and care over the next months and years, and intuitively recognized my need for support.

Even in grief, even at that young age, I knew I had to seek a path forward. I was very concerned about how our family was going to get through this. I was so fortunate that Annette's care showed me proof of how a large, close-knit family would be my answer. From that night on, I realized that family was going to get me through, and I was given deep insight into the importance of rallying around those who are experiencing loss and pain. That was the very beginning of my path to helping others.

Thirty-plus years later, Jen is still one of my closest friends, and though Annette is no longer with us, I will be eternally grateful for her love and the outpouring of affection from their family that inspired me to move my life in a positive direction and build a strong family of my own.

Losing my brother is one of the hardest things that has ever happened to me. And yet, this tragic event taught me the most valuable truth: Life is precious and short, so live it full out. My early appreciation of the power of family love—nuclear and extended family, including our families of friends—has given my life meaning, and helps to keep Michael's memory close. For that, I'll always be grateful.

LIFE COACHING AND JOURNALING

What Is a Life Coach?

I am a life coach.

Maybe you're thinking, what is that?

A life coach is a professional trained to help people with what most of us struggle with at some point in our lives and to various degrees: moving our lives forward and reaching our goals, whatever they may be. A life coach is a person who listens, motivates, inspires, and holds you accountable. Someone who invites you to ask hard questions about yourself—and asks you hard questions right back.

Life coaches don't give advice and they don't solve your problems. This is not therapy; it is purposeful, measurable communication, and there are no easy solutions to the kinds of things they address. What some coaches do, myself included, may be even more valuable in taking control of your life: We ask permission to ask you questions—and as you work to answer them, your path forward begins to be revealed.

With the help of a life coach, you can create the space you need to let in important personal and professional insights. With these insights, you can make choices—and those choices will move you in a positive direction, toward what I like to call your Best Version.

When writing this book, my goal was to do two things: 1) Share my life story with you, openly and honestly, chapter by chapter, with full transparency. This was crucial to me because I am living proof that each of us is capable of astonishing transformation. And 2) Help you experience how amazing it feels to change your life by changing your choices, and to embark on a journey that never ends.

In my daily life, my overall goal is to help others create positive change in their lives, to motivate and inspire them to embrace possibility. And here's a confession for you: I also wrote this book for me, to remind myself how I got through my own challenges and to create a document I can always refer to, to keep myself going. As you read the lessons, keep in mind that while you should strive to follow them every day, the striving is exactly that—always a work in progress. Our lives are never going to be perfect. I just know that these lessons are the bedrock that supports my life and they are always there to help me when I hit a bump in the road. They ground me, they move me, and they inspire me. They never fail to help me. And I believe they will do the same for you.

Journaling

I am a passionate believer that journaling, taking time to capture your thoughts in words and write them down with pen and paper or whatever medium you prefer, is a vital tool for the process of moving in a positive direction in life. For the program in this book, to focus the substance and intentions of each Life Lesson and make them really approachable and attainable, and to help you clarify your thoughts, each chapter ends with a series of relevant questions designed for reflection—called ThinkWork. This is where journaling comes into the picture.

Simple as it is, journaling in some form every day has been the single most effective tool I've used over the years to reflect upon, design, and maintain the life I now love. The process of writing down our thoughts and trying to express them clearly helps us understand ourselves. In that way, it has absolutely been instrumental in helping me work toward the life and outcomes I desire. All you need is a pen and a simple notebook. For those of you who are new to journaling, go easy on yourself and stay flexible; the only rule is, do it every day. Some of you may find you enjoy writing a few (or many) pages, while others might only need to put down a few words or phrases that have meaning for you.

If you don't like the idea of writing on paper, there are many options for documenting your thoughts. You can use your smartphone to record audio or even video of your thoughts. I write on everything—if I'm in the car, I might use a napkin or a sticky note. I definitely use the record button on my phone. Whatever it takes, whatever method you use, the idea is to be able to revisit those thoughts and really listen to your own words. I have been journaling since I was a kid and I still have all of my notebooks. I love going back and reading entries from years ago and realizing how far I've come.

Along with deepening our understanding of ourselves and opening doors to new insights, recording our thoughts helps us gradually build up trust in our own instincts. It's a lot like developing core strength during workouts: Just as we feel in flow when we're moving and exercising, listening to our thoughts helps get us in tune with ourselves.

So, use the ThinkWork questions as prompts to start writing in a journal. And keep at it—developing a habit takes time (often not that long), and once you do, you may be surprised how much you like it.

MOVING TOWARD YOUR GOALS

The first question I want you to ask yourself is, Am I moving toward or away from my goals?

Before you can answer this, of course, you need to know what your goals are.

Goals come in all shapes and sizes, and the beauty of that is it means you can start with small goals and work your way up to something bigger. For me, every day starts with setting a goal. Food shopping may seem like a small, ordinary goal, often probably more like a chore. So when I need to get food shopping done for my family, I tell myself, "My goal this morning is to get to the market." I remind myself that even though it may feel like a chore, it's way more than that. It's something that you want to achieve, and anything worth achieving is a goal.

On days when I wake up with low energy, I sometimes give myself permission to put aside my bigger goals—like working on my next book or article or creating a new coaching opportunity—and stick to addressing smaller ones that actually feel like they can be achieved that day: making calls, returning emails, doing laundry, doing the dishes, making doctors' appointments, cleaning up after the kids. Setting out to achieve these smaller things is part of focusing on goals—and putting just some, not all, of the little ones on your list is okay, too. It's important to keep your expectations realistic, to set yourself up for success.

Now, for the big stuff. Defining life goals can seem overwhelming, sometimes (or a lot of the time), for pretty much all of us. Especially if you're young and choosing your direction, or are transitioning between careers or to midlife, or from kids to empty nest. Maybe you're unhappy with your situation and don't really know why. Even if you're on what seems like a fine track, you might have conflicting desires or be feeling a shift in priorities. Review any bigger goals you have once or twice a year. There's no need to dwell on or obsess about them. Just carve out time around the new year or maybe in September when the end of summer and the start of school offers you a nice spot to pause and review your weightier goals. We'll be digging into how to define our larger goals as we move through the Life Lessons ahead.

All goals, any goals, give structure, movement, balance, and meaning to our days, and the accumulation of those days is our life. Every time we accomplish a goal, large or small, that's our reminder that we are in flow and creating positive change.

So, how do you know if you are moving closer to your goals, or farther away? There is one surefire way to find out: Notice—really notice—your feelings around the concept we can call progress. When you move toward a goal, you will be able to measure—actually measure—your progress. That is, you will feel your energy build; you will have a sense of hope. When you feel defeated, heavy, lethargic, or even hopeless, you may look for (and find) circumstantial things to explain it. Feelings like that are definitely a red flag that you're moving away from a goal that is important to you. Pay attention to your feelings on both ends of the range and learn to recognize when you have them.

In between a sense of vital or rising energy and an absence of energy, there's a frustrating phenomenon: the feeling of treading water. Nothing is worse than expending energy and not moving. This is another reminder that our goals are our guiding lights. They tell us what actions we want to take. However, they don't just come to us; that's why we need to set our goals mindfully, thoughtfully, measurably, and then act on them.

Finally, it's important to recognize that it's in the nature of goals to change over time. Goals are absolutely fluid: They change as we grow and our circumstances evolve. Starting as a young child, my most fervent goal was to pursue politics as a career. I carried it all the way to college, where I chose to become a political science major as a way to continue moving toward that goal. However, after a year of study and struggle with the course material (I'm mildly to moderately dyslexic, so reading the analyses of complex global relationships in the field and numerous subfields and understanding them was a huge challenge for me), I was ready to make a change. I realized political science was not going to be the best major for my skill set, and I changed my goal. My values didn't change—I was still focused on serving others, as I am today. What changed was how I would live my values. It's only when we begin to move toward a goal that we can evaluate whether or not to continue on the path, or alter it. Setting a goal does not mean we have to live with it forever. It's something we move toward, and if it feels right, we keep moving toward it—and if it doesn't feel right, we create a new one.

For example, you may feel at some point in your life that you want to move across the country and live in a place that's entirely different from where you grew up. As you get older, though, you may start to appreciate the significance of family—of being close to your roots, to siblings and aging parents, of having the support of and identification with your network, community, or tribe. That goal of moving far away may start to lose its appeal. When that happens, it's time to reset your goal to create your life's new road map.

I'll say it again: It's important to remember that goals are always fluid—and you made them, so be open to changing them without guilt. That is the challenge: knowing what you want to get from the day, the week, the month, a year. All that takes time, energy, and planning. If you do the work laid out in the Life Lessons I gathered into this book, I promise you will make better decisions that move you toward the things you ultimately want in life.

HOW TO USE THIS BOOK

Throughout the pages of this book, you'll see I repeat a number of phrases and terms which have become part of my standard teaching vocabulary to identify and talk about concepts in the lessons. I'll define them briefly below. When you encounter them in the context of the lessons, you can refer back here if needed. Once they become familiar you can use them as touchstones and as quick reminders of what you've learned.

Do List. As I mentioned before, goals can be big or small or anything in between. I like to put my small goals on a "Do List"—not a to-do list. Though it may seem like a fine point of difference, when you put small goals on a Do List, it's a call to action: Now. Goals on a Do List are those you plan to accomplish that day . . . okay, maybe the next. If you think about it, often our to-do lists are really a list of things that need doing sometime, who knows when. Once you feel the difference, a Do List will spur you on to more immediate action. Put boxes next to the entries and check them off as you complete them. You'll feel great every time you slap a checkmark on the list. I guarantee it.

Best Version. I use the term Best Version to describe the person you want to be. It's you living the combination of all your goals. Working toward this is a lifelong process. While there will always be hard days, there will also be days when you feel like you truly are living the way you want to, and when you do, notice it, appreciate it, learn from it; you are moving toward your Best Version.

The Four C's. My mission as a life coach is to help my clients connect, communicate, collaborate, and change in a positive direction. I use these four words all the time, as these factors are the cornerstones of my coaching practice.

Think It. Write It. Share It. I use a three-step model for my basic approach to manifesting goals.

1   *Think It.* This is about that little voice you hear in your head every day. Amidst all the clamor of daily necessity, ideas come to us. Some we dismiss, some we play out. These are the thoughts we can learn to grab onto—the things we dream about, the visions in our head. The trick is to be open and listen to them. Your thoughts are where goals are born.

Where are you usually when you come up with your best, clearest ideas? For me, it's when I'm moving: on a mat doing yoga, meditating, or taking a long walk without the distraction of music (my thoughts are my mental music). One of my clients has her best ideas in the shower. Once you've identified your best thinking place, make it part of your regular practice to go there, even if it's only for a few minutes. Have you ever been right in the middle of doing something ordinary and an amazing new idea pops into your head? Find the place where that happened and go back to it.

2 *Write It.* Ever since I was a kid, journaling has been my favorite mode of expression, and I still have dozens of boxes filled with journals dating from the fourth grade on. The early ones detail dates, breakups, feelings of heartache and despair—basically every kiss and emotion, success and failure. I've saved these diaries because I really feel like they are the road map of my journey. By the time I was in my twenties, I was writing about what I wanted from my life (a career, home, and family), in words and also with drawings. All this allowed me to see my goals like a map, and helped enable me to make the decisions that would move me toward those targets, toward the life I wanted. Those hand-written volumes are where I believe my coaching practice began: I was coaching myself.

It's simple. When you put pen or pencil to paper and write down your intentions, you solidify them—make them physical and in that way make them real. Then you can start planning how to make it happen. The possibilities are endless!

3 *Share It.* Once you have a goal and you've written it down, sharing is a wonderful way to hold yourself accountable. Talk about your goal with a friend or a family member. Even post it on social media. Once you think it and then write it, you should be ready to share, though you may want to pause here and make sure you're confident and ready to share. There's nothing quite like posting our intentions on Facebook, Instagram, or Twitter to keep us committed to pursuing a goal to completion and fresh reminders that it's worth it.

Live Directionally. If your Best Version is the destination, then living directionally is the journey. It's the feeling of movement: the ride as you move forward in the process.

Want versus Need. In the context of this program, "want" is a positive, motivating word that drives us to take action. "I want" moves you toward your goals, whereas "I need" can feel and sound tentative, fearful, dependent, desperate—even debilitating. Think about it: Being needy is usually perceived as a negative, while wanting something expresses a positive, confident desire.

And versus But. Throughout the text of this book, I have actively avoided using the word "but." Of course it's a hardworking conjunction for sentence structure, but (see!) it's often used in contexts where a negative implication comes out, intentionally or not, and just saying it can bring you down and even effectively cancel out everything you just said prior. "And" links thoughts together, encourages connection, and takes you forward. Try paying attention to this subtle difference when you speak, listen, and write and make the small changes; I think you'll see how it positively moves you!

ThinkWork. This is my version of homework—homework for grownups. It's the thinking plus the work that takes place as you read the Life Lessons, meditate on and digest the instruction and new concepts, and begin to apply the lessons to your own life circumstances.

IT'S ONLY A PROBLEM IF YOU MAKE IT A PROBLEM

EVERYONE STRUGGLES. SOME PROBLEMS SEEM IMPOS-sible, like financial struggles, divorce, illness, and death, and should be tackled slowly and methodically. Others are smaller, like disagreeing with your children on what to eat for dinner each night, or arguing about who should take out the trash. Sometimes, we create

NEVER BE
AFRAID TO
MOVE FORWARD
THROUGH ANY
PERCEIVED
OBSTACLE.

Look at any momentary setback as an opportunity to flex your problem-solving muscle.

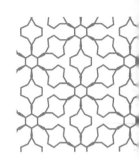

problems for ourselves, and they're not really problems. I hear people complain about rescheduling appointments and meetings—these are not problems; they are decisions that need to be made. What about the friend who panics, "My son can't take his driving test today!" While this might be unfortunate and disappointing, the probability is high that there's another day he can take his test. Panicking about it merely puts an obstacle in your day that doesn't need to be there. Never be afraid to move forward through any perceived obstacle. Look at any momentary setback as an opportunity to flex your problem-solving muscle.

I understand loss, divorce, and addiction are enormous challenges. So many of us deal with these issues and they are huge—I've experienced all three. However, even faced with issues that seem insurmountable, you can make small adjustments to steer your life in a different direction, yielding big, positive results.

Do you long to be a better version of yourself? Do you want love . . . hope . . . success? Then get ready to make some hard decisions. The

5 SMALL CHANGES I MADE IN MY OWN LIFE

- Eliminate late-night snacking
- Exercise 30 minutes each day
- Go to sleep early (usually before 10 p.m.)
- Limit TV time
- Cap any alcohol consumption to 2 drinks a day, and keep 2 to 3 days per week alcohol free

What would your list of small changes look like? Think about it, write it down, and get ready to commit to each one.

first is to stop labeling things a problem! If it were easy, everyone would do it. It's going to take tremendous discipline; it requires serious commitment. As your coach, I'm here to say, I know you can do it.

Very often, when we want to achieve a large life shift or meet an important goal, it's best to start with small, attainable steps before moving on to bigger ones. If you want to purchase a home, for example, the first step isn't calling a broker, it's getting your finances in order, doing the research, and possibly securing a loan. If you want to find a new job, the first step isn't to contact the desired employer, it's to get your resume in order. Each of these first steps should be attainable goals on your DO list. (I never say TO DO—the Glosserman method is simply, DO.)

Small goals, such as checking items off your DO list, give instant gratification. They are a fantastic way to move your life toward positivity, enabling you to have the energy, momentum, and confidence needed to achieve those bigger goals. Think of something little that you've always wanted to change, and make that your goal today. It can be as simple as just getting up earlier in the morning. Recently, I moved my wake-up time from 7 a.m. to 6—and it's had an incredibly positive impact on how I feel and perform each day. That one extra hour has given me much needed "me" time to prepare for my clients, meditate, and organize before my family awakens and places natural demands on my time. By actually getting up one hour earlier, I proved to myself that I could set a goal and achieve it. I could have complained that I never had enough time for my clients or for me—I could have made this a problem. Instead, I chose not to. I added this small goal to my DO list, found a solution, and made it work for me, and it felt amazing. And, that feeling of accomplishment gave me momentum that I could use to build toward larger goals.

Often we do things out of habit, yet we don't consider why we made those decisions in the first place. We are on automatic pilot. It can be challenging to recognize when patterns no longer serve us. The next

Remember, I never say TO DO—the Glosserman method is simply, DO.

Most of us have "problems" with romantic relationships. When I ultimately met *the* guy, he was different from what I envisioned, and yet very much what I needed. Things don't always come in the packages that we box ourselves into. My husband, Marc, is levelheaded and very intelligent. I was used to being with alpha males, the big athletic football player type. Marc is caring and kind. Instantly we had a very strong connection. Despite that instant connection, he told me immediately that he didn't want to marry a smoker, even a casual one, and at that point in my life, I was lighting up regularly. "I adore you," confessed the man I'd waited so long to meet. "But I don't think I could live with a smoker." This could have been a real problem. My unhealthy habit could have stood in the way of my healthy future and the loving relationship I'd always wanted.

I made a choice: to DO something about it. I committed to quitting smoking. I realized that smoking has several consequences, and the consequence of losing Marc was far greater than my desire for a cigarette. Smoking cessation is one of the hardest things anyone can do: it's a serious addiction. I began to quit one small step at a time, and here's how:

First, I decided I would only smoke two cigarettes a day. Believe me, this was really difficult. Every day, I would reinforce my goals: I wanted to be healthy and I wanted to be with Marc. This was my mantra. Once I was able to do that—it took a couple of months—I went down to two cigarettes per week. Months later, I finally reached that wonderful day when I knew I was done. I literally taught myself to quit smoking. And it was hard—anyone who's tried to kick smoking (or any addiction) knows that all too well. I looked at what had worked for me in the past, and I relied on my mantras. When I was able to appreciate that all those things that I wanted were stronger than my desire to smoke, my attitude toward "giving up" something I'd become accustomed to changed, and quitting smoking became a positive goal that I could realistically achieve. I no longer felt like I was giving up anything. Instead I was gaining something much more important. The act of reminding myself every day of what I wanted allowed me to reinforce my choice and make it happen.

This is how I chose to quit smoking and it worked for me. How you do it could be very different. Whatever you do, never be afraid to ask for help. There are many resources out there to help stop smoking. All you need is the right one and the right support system and you can do it too.

time you are engaged in a pattern that no longer serves you, ask your-self: Why am I making this choice? Is this choice moving me toward what I want, or away from it?

Sometimes people create problems that aren't even there. It happens all the time and I laugh when I catch myself doing it. Aren't there enough problems in this world, without our having to invent nonexistent ones? Again, I see this all the time in romantic relationships. Couples allow their differences to become obstacles when in fact it was most likely those differences that drew them together in the first place. I'll give another example. My husband, Marc, is Jewish and I was raised Catholic. Early in the relationship, he expressed the importance of having a Jewish home—which meant raising our children in the Jewish faith. That could have been a problem—and sadly, it's an obstacle that some couples simply cannot overcome. I chose not to make it a problem because I realized my goal was to be in a loving relationship

Aren't there enough problems in this world, without our having to invent nonexistent ones?

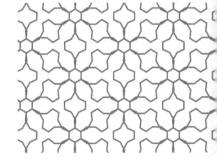

and have a family with Marc, and for me, that was the most important thing. So I took his strongest value and embraced it. I spent over a year studying Judaism at the 92nd Street Y, a New York City landmark. Once I discovered for myself that Judaism is a profound belief system anchored in centuries of beautiful tradition, I realized it was in tune with my own lifelong love of spirituality. Although I never did convert (never say never!), I now have a deep appreciation and respect for our family's chosen religion. Our four children are all Jewish. And as it turns out, our two youngest attended a Catholic school. Between their catechisms and prepping for my son's bar mitzvah, we were all immersed in a lot of religious study. Believe me, there's a lot of God in our home! And I believe that's a wonderful blessing.

I have always gravitated toward spirituality, even as a young child, long before I discovered the practice of yoga. Growing up, my Catholic parents rarely took us to church; still, we had a devout family tradition of displaying a crèche in the living room; ours was an heirloom with delicate ceramic figurines. Each piece of the Nativity was carefully wrapped up in tissue paper for storage after the holiday; by early December, I was counting down the days for my Mom to unpack them, piece by piece, and display the Nativity scene. My favorite figure was the Baby Jesus, and as soon as He was unwrapped, I would cradle Him in my hands, just like an Easter egg, and—also like an Easter egg—I would hide Him! I would not let anyone else have a peek at the Baby Jesus until the time of his birth: Christmas Eve at the stroke of midnight. My mother was a former Catholic school teacher, and I could see she approved of my enthusiasm.

Like the crèche in the living room, it has always been important to me to keep an element of hope and possibility in the home I've created with Marc—and I believe that for all of us, religion and religious articles are very accessible vehicles for hope and possibility. I'll take God wherever God can be found: in a cathedral or a temple . . . out in nature . . . on a mountaintop or at a beach. At times of crisis, faith can give us all an outlet, a tool we can use to process challenging information. I saw faith get many people through difficult challenges—it got me through the death of my brother—and I can relate to leaning on God in times of need.

We're all faced with challenges in life: We can choose to focus on the negative and create problems for ourselves, which will only bring us down and add to our unhappiness. Or we can choose to move toward

THINKWORK

- Where in your life are you making a problem where there doesn't need to be one?
- Think back to a time when you allowed something to become a problem. Identify the obstacle and how you'd approach it differently today.

the positive in all things. When we approach life as a series of challenges, as obstacles we're excited to overcome, we experience a shift toward possibility and positive change.

Remember, it's only a problem if you make it a problem. It's your choice.

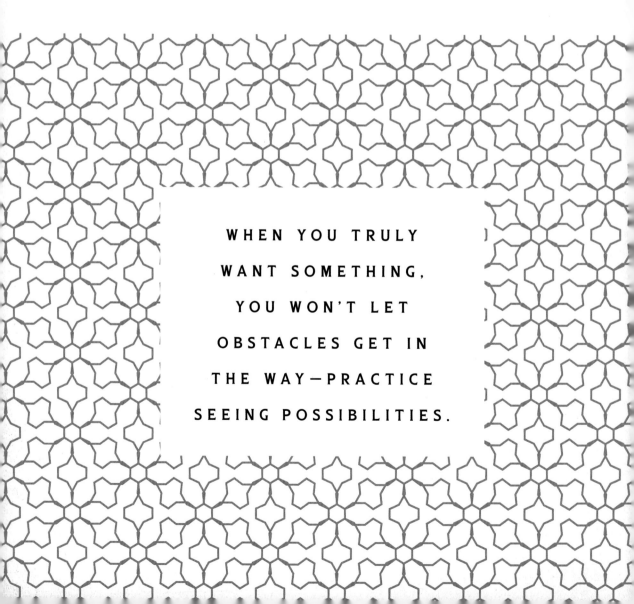

WHEN YOU TRULY WANT SOMETHING, YOU WON'T LET OBSTACLES GET IN THE WAY—PRACTICE SEEING POSSIBILITIES.

2

BEGIN. FOCUS. COMMIT.

ONE OF THE THINGS I HEAR MOST FROM MY CLIENTS is that they want to make a change and they just don't know where to begin. I have found, in my own long journey, that there's a relatively easy way to overcome that first obstacle—and guess what? I call it "Begin." I know you've heard it a million times and the truth is, it's true. Although changing your life can be hard, you can start by taking one simple, small step forward.

BEGIN

Try this: At night, before you go to sleep, tell yourself how you're going to begin the next day. It's just like preparing for a meeting, only you are meeting with your own intention. By deciding what you will do the very first thing in the morning, you can control how your day begins instead of the day controlling you. This is a discipline that I encourage you to practice until it becomes a habit. When you start the day with intention, you will feel empowered with purpose, with a clear and positive path.

For me, begin often means doing something physical first thing in the morning. Sometimes I walk around the block by myself, do sun salutations in my living room, or meditate for two minutes in the bathroom. If I'd like to concentrate on training, I hit the basement gym.

Other days, I might check an item off my Do List, such as making a call I've been putting off, writing a response to an overdue email, or composing a thank-you note that's been on my mind.

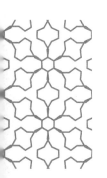

By deciding what you will do the very first thing in the morning, you can control how your day begins instead of the day controlling you.

Think about how you can start each morning with a small accomplishment that will set the tone for the rest of the day. The key is to set your intention and follow through. It may take a while to develop this habit, so be patient, and begin. You'll be glad you did.

Here are some things I do to begin my day to set myself up for confident intention:

- Sit down with a cup of coffee and take some quiet time to create my Do List.
- Ten yoga sun salutations.
- Call my mom or dad or another family member or friend I've been thinking about.
- Pay a bill.
- Meditate.

What kinds of things could you do to begin your day with clear intention? Start small, with just one thing, and stick to it in those early moments when the whirl of activity often can carry us away. Take a 10-minute walk, or schedule an appointment you've been putting off. This simple approach to beginning the day will set you up for a productive day ahead. Over time, instead of that scattered feeling of turning off your alarm and wondering what to tackle first after the coffee is made, it will feel totally natural to begin your day with purpose and intention.

FOCUS

Think about focus as a frame for your whole day. I've found that when I'm really on track and getting things done, it's because I have chosen a specific focus or theme for my day. Think of it as a large brushstroke: Focus doesn't tell you what to do specifically; it simply reminds you where you want the majority of your energy to go. This approach to the concept of focus can keep you on track all day.

Let's say today your focus is on your family. In that case, you might create a plan that allows you to book doctor appointments, order the kids' school/sports/hobby supplies, and respond to teachers' emails, making sure to work these tasks into your already busy schedule.

When you choose your focus, keep in mind you are not trying to devote the whole day to one area of life. You still have to work, plan meals, and run errands. Maybe you have a dog, and they'll need

EYE ON THE PRIZE

Things I choose to focus on for a day:
- Finances
- Job growth and career
- Relationships
- Family and kids
- Health
- Self-care (Don't skip this one—it's so important to make time to focus on yourself!)

When you name your focus, you'll have a clear reminder of which tasks you should be concentrating on today.

your attention. You surely have dozens of other items on your internal checklist. By focusing the day on one category of accomplishment, however, you'll get more things done—just by mitigating distraction. We all have a tendency to veer off course: You might have a complicated project you need to work on at the office, or you might just lose track of time looking through old photos or cleaning out your closet. Or you might be checking Instagram once too often. When you name your focus, you'll have a clear reminder of which tasks you should be concentrating on today. And at the end of the day, the same clear frame lets you look back and see the progress you made—and that will give you the momentum and encouragement you need to focus on tomorrow's tasks. This begins to put you in a positive cycle.

COMMIT

The last element in this chapter's triumvirate of power points is commit. Begin. Focus. Commit. Let these be your mantra.

I've noticed that in times of stress, I tend to neglect myself. Even if I have a plan to begin my day and I have named my focus, I still have to carry through a commitment. So to take care of myself, using the lesson in this chapter, I commit to making sure that no matter how much I "need" to get done, no matter how demanding my kids are, no matter how much I want to support my husband, I have to do something for myself. It can be something small. Maybe an hour (or half an hour!) with the book I've been dying to read, or that hike I've been meaning to check out. Sometimes there's almost no time at all, so even ten minutes alone in the bathroom can help.

When I was writing this book, I maintained stability by being my own coach and making a daily promise to myself: Do one or a few things to keep me on schedule, grounded, and focused. As long as I committed to that, I could give 100 percent of myself to my family for the rest of the day. To understand commit purposefully in this context, think of it as naming the one thing you absolutely commit yourself to achieving today. Even if you accomplish nothing else, at the end of the day, your commit should be completed.

Even if you accomplish nothing else, at the end of the day, your commit should be completed.

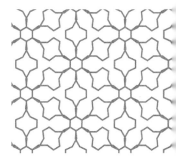

Movement is incredibly important to me, so very often my commit is to work out. I try to do that several mornings each week. There are days when crossing something off our DO list does more than take care of business—it also provides great peace of mind. That's why I firmly believe that we should prioritize our own needs ahead of all those other pressures of daily life. First, we must allocate time to ourselves for space and self-care. For me, the first priority is my workouts. For you, it might be reading, writing, painting, baking, stretching, getting outside, meditation, music. I think about it like being on an airplane and listening to the safety briefing. The first thing they stress is to put the oxygen mask on your own face before helping others—even your own kids. To have the energy to take care of others, you must nurture yourself first. So be sure to commit to the one thing: Take a bath, play with the dog, practice an instrument, exercise . . . and next time, when you are feeling stressed or overwhelmed, stop for a minute and commit yourself to a little more me time.

Your commit can also be a good place to check off a nagging task on your list that you've been avoiding. In my case, I'm not so good with technology, so if I want to get something done on the computer, I tend to avoid it or put it last on the list. Instead, I now place those items at the top of my list and I commit to getting them done. You will be amazed at how good it feels to take a not-so-fun item off your list. Give it a try!

KEEP MOVING!

Exercise—any kind of moving your body—can happen anywhere. Even when weather interferes and we can't get to the gym, there are plenty of options indoors. During the long months of sheltering in place and/or quarantining during the Covid-19 crisis, I had to get creative, because I like to go running or take long walks and that wasn't always possible. So, I started doing yoga in my room, and I joined streaming video fitness classes. I could have used the pandemic as an excuse to avoid exercising. Instead I knew I needed to keep it going for me. That is why I continued to commit to this time: I knew it would keep me grounded and fully present for my family and my clients for the rest of the day.

And it worked (and as I always say, do what works) because when we took the time to plan, we still had ample time to get everyone breakfast and clean up and make sure all the kids got online and were engaged in their classes. Then Marc could go and take his calls. Late morning or just before lunch turned out to be the perfect interval for me to take my time without taking anything away from anyone else. Letting go of any guilt about taking time for yourself is not just okay, it's essential. Making commitments to ourselves is key to prioritizing what we want as we steer toward our goals.

When you commit and actually follow through, you learn how to keep a promise to yourself. This builds and strengthens integrity within you and gives validity and honor to the words you choose. Commit helps you move toward your very Best Version (see page 20).

Make a list of things you'd like to commit to, day by day. They don't need to be big; they just must be important to you. Start with small things, like getting the rent check in the mail or making that mammogram appointment. Just make sure it's something you can complete. As you build a consistent daily practice of choosing to commit and following through no matter what, try adding things

When you commit and actually follow through, you learn how to keep a promise to yourself.

WAYS TO COMMIT

Here are a few commits I've put on my daily list over the years:

- Exercise—running or yoga.
- Go the entire day without raising my voice.
- Make a new recipe for dinner at home.
- Do my own taxes (that was a hard one!).
- Take a webinar or online class.
- Clean out the playroom or garage.
- Update my website and other social media profiles.

THINKWORK

- List three ways you can begin your day with intention.
- Describe a focus for your day that will fuel you and make you feel purposeful, productive, and inspired.
- What would you like to finally get done right now that will free you and make you feel lighter? Commit to it!

that are a bit bigger to that list. When you commit, you will always go to sleep knowing you got something positive done that day. An even bigger reason to commit is that you are holding yourself responsible, and that is very powerful. Every time you commit to something and do it, you will deepen your trust in yourself to do it again and again. Soon you will be so confident and attuned to the process, you'll be ready to accomplish anything!

A while ago, I was thinking about running a half marathon. I hadn't done one in nearly eight years, and every time I thought about the possibility of doing another, I got excited. Finally, on a lovely summer evening, we were out with some friends for dinner. One of the people with us shared that he'd just signed up for a half marathon. Immediately I said, "I'm in!" And at that moment, I knew there was no looking back: I had shared my intention with someone I really respected. I had said it out loud and now it was real. There was no way I was going back on my word.

I ran that half marathon using the concepts in this chapter: Begin. Focus. Commit. Commit in particular helps me mark milestones, no matter what distance I have ahead of me! We've all had those moments where we feel like we're on a treadmill and can't seem to get anywhere. We're simply moving, just not toward our goal. Commit allows you to take a step in a new forward direction, every time. How's that for measurable progress?

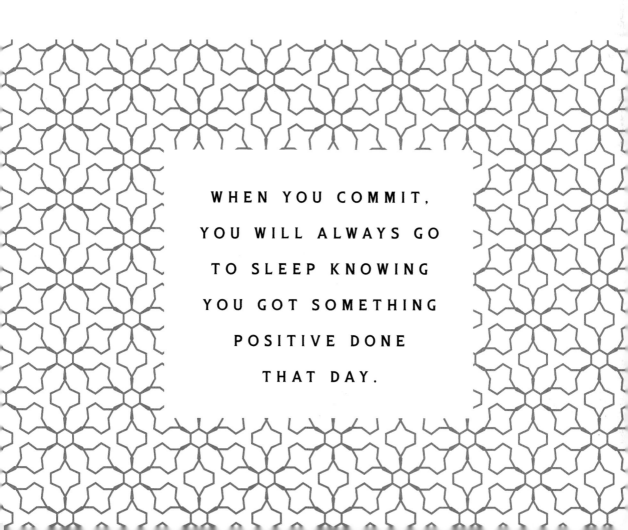

WHEN YOU COMMIT, YOU WILL ALWAYS GO TO SLEEP KNOWING YOU GOT SOMETHING POSITIVE DONE THAT DAY.

CHANGE IS HARD AND CHANGE IS GOOD

"CHANGE IS THE ONLY CONSTANT IN LIFE," SAID the philosopher Heraclitus. This idea is timeless and absolute. It takes most people years, even a lifetime, to accept this concept. Embracing change is a big step toward actively moving yourself toward new goals. When an unforeseen thing happens, it can be very uncomfortable, even paralyzing. When that thing is a sudden reversal or upheaval like a family death, a marriage dissolving, or the end of a career, it can be completely overwhelming. Oddly, even good changes are scary for many people, because we're facing the unfamiliar. I believe you must embrace change or you'll spend all your time fighting it, which will create more unwanted distance between you, your goals, and the life you want.

Life throws us challenges and obstacles all the time, and we don't always have control over what they are or when they will happen. What if you suddenly lost your job? That's a huge change, possibly devastating. It may feel like you have two main choices: You can lament the blow and complain to your friends while being angry at your employer, which will do nothing, really, to solve your situation. Or, you could take a moment and look for opportunity within. Maybe this is your chance to apply for that great job you always wanted, but you were always too busy working to dust off your resume. Think about your goals, your vision for what you want your life to be, and decide

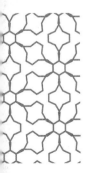

Think about your goals, your vision for what you want your life to be, and decide if this change could lead to something you really want.

if this change could lead to something you really want. Then you can make positive steps toward those goals.

By embracing change, you will be better able to make thoughtful, strategic decisions, feel more confident about the direction you are heading in, and begin to experience different outcomes, including the ones you actually want and choose. Your positive, intentional choices will lead you where you really want to go.

This transformation in attitude toward change probably won't happen overnight. Change can be like a dripping faucet, or it can be a tidal wave. The important thing is to keep moving forward in your intended direction. Then even when you're having hard days—and we all have them—you have a strategy in place that will actively help you create a different outcome. This new perspective will give you the tools you need when adversity strikes or you're feeling fear of the unknown. You will be able to safely say, "Okay, I'm in this moment—how am I going to deal with it positively? What can I do differently? What can I change?"

HAVING A GAME PLAN AND PUTTING POINTS ON THE BOARD

I've always loved sports and in school I played them all: soccer, tennis, lacrosse, and swimming. Today, I am a life coach in private practice, giving inspirational talks to parents and professionals, with two successful businesses. I still use my love and knowledge of sports

GETTING UNSTUCK

My life changed dramatically when I finally opened myself up to certain possibilities in the world instead of shutting myself off from them, and I made a conscious decision to shift away from my old stuck patterns and thoughts.

When I was thirty years old, I was pretty close to hitting rock bottom. I was getting divorced and depressed, and I had no career direction. I had a good job in sales, and I was making a good living, yet I knew I wasn't inspired. Living in Manhattan made me happy and I made enough money to pay my bills, enjoy a great social life, and come home to an adorable studio apartment—what's not to like, right? However, I was not doing what I enjoyed most: helping people.

Along the way, I hadn't realized what was missing. I started to fill that void in my life with other distractions. I became overly concerned with getting married quickly. I thought a partner and children would fill the emptiness (a thought pattern so many of us slide into), and I dove headfirst into relationships I didn't truly care about. I was drinking too much and not making good decisions. I was out of personal alignment, and I wasn't taking the time to honor my values or think about what I truly wanted.

I knew something was not right, yet I was afraid to make a change.

Finally, I made myself take the time to look closely at my life and break it down. My work satisfied basic needs, so it made sense as a choice; though I had to admit, it just wasn't getting me where I wanted to go. Was I really doing what I wanted to be doing? Or was I just killing time and punching a clock? Under honest scrutiny, it became obvious that it was a job, not a calling. Without noticing, I had drifted away from my goals: to inspire, to motivate, and, above all, to help others. And it showed. At that point, I couldn't even help myself.

I'm sure you know how easy it is to get diverted from your goals. When I graduated from college, the message wasn't "Live your dream!" or "Create the best version of yourself!" It was, "Get out there and get a job." Things were just different back then. So, when I was offered the job with Xerox, I turned my back on a possible creative position in media with *GQ* magazine because it seemed like a smarter and safer choice. Unfortunately, I quickly realized that the job was not going to bring me the personal and professional fulfillment I was seeking. Already, I was struggling with the classic trap—feeling like it was too late to change. I figured that was just how "adult" life was.

So, I got married and that wasn't the answer. It didn't fill the empty space, and with a too hasty marriage on top of an unfulfilling job, I felt even more lost. One summer night, my constant unhappiness led me to stay up watching pre-dawn infomercials. I was feeling trapped, powerless, and hopeless, particularly about my relationship and my career. And that's when Tony Robbins came on the TV. He seemed to know exactly what he was meant to do with his life, and I was fascinated. What he was saying really resonated with me. I jumped online and started searching keywords: motivation . . . teaching . . . coaching . . . training. That very night, I felt my mindset change, I felt myself willing to open my mind, and I realized that the only way out of my current situation was to change my path—and myself—by establishing new goals and making choices that would take my life in a completely new direction.

The first step for me was to focus on my job. To create true positive change, I needed to find a job that I cared about—one that would support me emotionally as well as financially. I set a small, achievable goal to get started and move me in that direction. And that was to apply for any job that was closer to my ultimate passion. Doing this was hard—and it was good.

I made sure I was open to whatever change came my way. Next thing I knew, I was walking into an Equinox flagship location, where I was offered the job of manager of sales operations on the spot. That confirmation of my ability to change directions was a huge boost to my confidence. Although I didn't end up staying there for very long, I had taken a very positive step by using one of my passions—fitness—to get a job that combined something that brings me joy with a reasonable salary. Once I knew I could find a job that made me feel good every day, in an environment with happy people, I had the mental space to focus on my larger goal: building my own consulting career as a coach.

every day. I have always been a serious competitor, and I love how in sports, it's always easy to see if you're doing well by how many points you have on the scoreboard. Success in sports is always clearly defined. Defining success in life coaching can be a little harder, although the common denominator is the constant work toward your goal. Success means you've reached the goal you set for yourself. You can check off that box and set some new goals. Score!

How do you know if you are moving closer to your goal or wandering farther away? One surefire way that works for me is to pay attention. Notice—really notice—how you feel as you make choices. When you are moving toward your goal, you will feel a sense of purpose and focused energy; you will have a sense of optimism and hope. When you move away from your goal, you might have feelings of heaviness

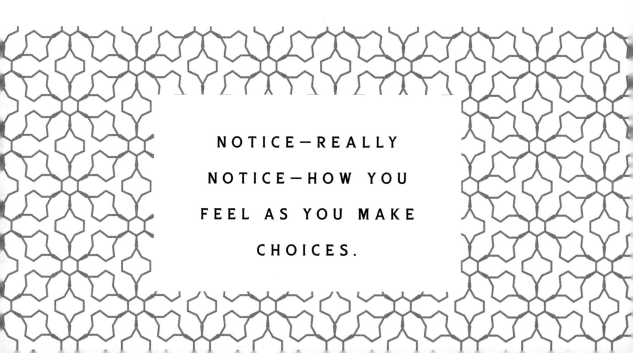

NOTICE—REALLY NOTICE—HOW YOU FEEL AS YOU MAKE CHOICES.

or lethargy. You may feel overwhelmed or even hopeless, as if whatever you do doesn't matter. You could have that frustrating feeling I mentioned earlier of treading water. Nothing is more soul-crushing than expending energy without making any progress. When you get feelings like that, pay attention. These are signs that should alert you to stop and reevaluate what you are doing. It may be time for you to make a change. And when you look back, you'll realize that when you noticed those feelings, that was your first step toward the new, positive goals that changed your life for the better.

When you are moving toward your goal, you will feel a sense of purpose and focused energy; you will have a sense of optimism and hope.

THINKWORK

- How do you feel about your life right now? Are you making progress?
- What in your life would you like to change? Where do you feel stuck?
- List three reasons why this change might be good for you.

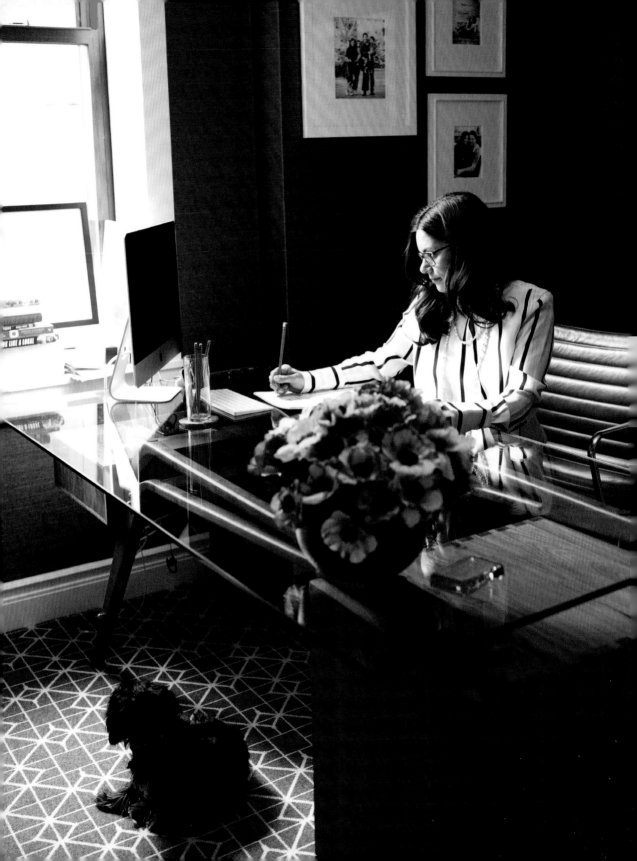

4

DO WHAT WORKS

BACK IN LESSON 1, I TALKED ABOUT HOW WE CAN unconsciously choose to create problems for ourselves, and how that makes life harder than it has to be. Instead of feeling—or even looking for—the negative, try stepping back from a situation and saying,

"Okay. What works?"

Can you think of a situation in your life that felt like an impossible uphill climb? Maybe you eventually surmounted it. Thinking back, can you see how you could have simplified things? That's really what this chapter's call to *do what works* is about: curbing the tendency to overcomplicate a situation or decision. Right now, the answer you're looking for could be right in front of you and more obvious than you think. Open your eyes and open your mind to seeing it.

Don't be distracted by any obstacles that stand in your way. Simply do what works for you in that moment. Think about something that you can do or change right now, even if it's small, all on your own. It could be as simple as deciding to stay home on Friday night instead of heading out to a bar or a social gathering after work. Stop overcomplicating your life's decisions. Take rest and downtime (or off time) when you need it. Stop listening to the noise and stop dwelling on "what if's." They will only suck up your energy and distract you from your goal.

Think about what works in your life. For you it could be getting more sleep during the week. Or getting in a solid habit of using a Do

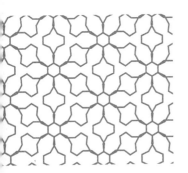

Right now, the answer you're looking for could be right in front of you and more obvious than you think.

MAKING HOME WORK

When Marc decided he was going to open our first restaurant, Hill Country Barbecue Market, in Manhattan, one of the things we did early on was to look for a place to live. We could have searched for a home near Central Park, the Upper West Side, or in Brooklyn, or even on Long Island. Instead I went on an apartment hunt and found a place within ten blocks of the restaurant. I think that single decision has everything to do with why, fourteen years later, Hill Country is still a successful business. Not only are we able to run back and forth between our home and our restaurant—and believe me, we do that a lot—we've actively built a personal community at the same time that is equally important to us. By paying attention to what works for our family, we found just the right place to be.

List (see page 19). In our family, once we had four kids, we realized that we wouldn't be able to travel as much as we used to. So we compromised by traveling to visit our families once or twice a year. It was less expensive and much easier logistically. We took what didn't work for us and turned it into something that would. Once you realize what works (and what doesn't), you might be surprised to find that other things will start falling into place. Recognizing what works and why (see Tools for Doing What Works below) will become a positive pattern in your daily life and bring you another step closer to your

TOOLS FOR DOING
WHAT WORKS

1. Identify what isn't working by checking in on your feelings. Negative feelings like stress or anxiety are key indicators that something is amiss.
2. Eliminate as many of the things that cause your negative feelings as possible—people pleasing, obligation, resentment, overextension. Don't make problems where none exist. Ask yourself if what you are doing is moving you toward your goal or away from it.

3. Create a Do List (see page 19) of "next steps." Each item should be small and doable in one day and should advance you toward your goal.

4. Take a look around your home and work environment. Are you living and working in an atmosphere in which your key needs are being met? It's really important to love the space you're in. Ask yourself: Are the desk and chair comfortable? Are the pillows soft? Do the colors make me happy? If I spot elements of my space that are dull or depressing or just don't suit me, I know it's time for a change. In my case, I always have a lot of fresh flowers around. For my husband, it's important to be surrounded by music, so his office has guitars and a Bruce Springsteen poster. Imagine yourself in your space. What elements would you add or change to make it a space that would make you happy?

5. Build and nurture a support system. Friends and family of course, or if you don't have a circle of friends where you are now or family nearby, try to cultivate friends and like-minded people, creatives, therapists, activists, fellow hobbyists, and the like through social media connections and word of mouth, et cetera. Coworkers who share common challenges or tradespeople who can help or barter with various burdens are also a great part of a support system.

6. Don't try to reinvent the wheel. You don't need to do everything yourself. ASK FOR HELP. You'll be glad you did.

ultimate goals and happiness. Meanwhile, some of the obstacles and negative thinking that may have been getting in your way are more likely to fall aside naturally because you have new insight into how you've been making problems where they don't really exist.

As you clear out the murkiness, confusion, or even chaos that has been distracting you, choosing what you want to do next will become even clearer, almost as if solutions and your next steps are presenting themselves to you. Of course, you'll still be confronted with challenges—that's just how life is—and that's when you'll use the tools here and in all the Life Lessons in this book and follow what works, which will make those issues much easier to resolve.

Sometimes it's hard to see what is working without eliminating what isn't. And as you've learned, you'll know what isn't working by the way you feel: You might be bored, irritated, anxious, or even have a sick feeling in your stomach that won't go away.

When you have trouble putting your thoughts into words, that's usually an indication that something's not working. When that happens, ask questions that clarify what you are feeling and try asking them right out loud:

"What am I solving for?"

"What is the outcome I'm looking for?"

"What can I do to make things easier?"

Immediately start making a Do List of actions that will move you toward your desired outcome, and write down whatever comes to

HELP CAN COME FROM ANYWHERE

If you are lucky, you have had a special teacher in your life who believed in you. Ms. Dorfman, my high school English teacher, was that person for me. She intuitively knew I had learning challenges, which we all came to understand as dyslexia. I struggled with my writing, and she understood that what I put down on paper was never as clear and compelling as my spoken ideas. She started planting seeds: "Did you ever think about public speaking? I could really see you as a news anchor." She encouraged me to try out for the speech and debate teams, and when I did, a whole world opened up to me. I'm so fortunate that Ms. Dorfman was aware of my challenges, saw my strengths, and offered me her help (I'm still working toward that talk show/on air opportunity). Look for that person in your life who can help you. It could be as close as a family member or as distant as a celebrity you look up to and read about and admire for their point of view. I would never have been able to get to where I am today without the help of some amazing people, every step of the way. I've learned that asking for help is a sign of strength, not weakness.

mind. Some might seem extreme or make you uncomfortable. One by one you can evaluate each idea and decide if it's truly unworkable or something worth exploring (so long as it's ethical: don't be robbing any banks to create personal wealth!). When I journal or make lists, I don't censor myself; I just let the ideas flow.

To help you do what works, again I emphasize that one of the most important things to do is build a community. I have no idea what I would do without my support system. Raising four children in New York isn't easy, so I've assembled a squad of caregivers, neighbors, family members, and friends who all help to make Team Glosserman work. I've never been shy about asking for help and neither should you.

To underscore my point, while the importance of self-sufficiency is healthy and a message we get from many corners of life, it's just as important when we are thinking about doing what works that we recognize that assistance can come from almost anywhere and is just as important for a strong and balanced support system. One such person could be your employer or a coworker. Does your supervisor or manager make you feel comfortable and capable? That person could help you discover what works and find places where you can stretch and excel.

Where in your life could you use a mentor or a guide of some sort to give you some direction? Whether it's your personal or professional life, don't be shy about asking: That's only going to up your game and make you better and stronger.

Don't be shy about asking: That's only going to up your game and make you better and stronger.

Once you feel you have your own support system in good shape, look at your family and make sure they have support, too. I have four beautiful children, and two of them are presenting with learning styles like mine. Every day, I encourage them to do what works—because that has always worked for me. I try to approach them from a positive angle by saying things like, "You're so bright, and I can see you are trying really hard. Would you like some extra help? You can count on me, your dad, and your siblings to help." As an example, I was frustrated once over some computer thing for about three weeks. My son, Austin, came over and managed it in three minutes flat. Now I never hesitate to ask him for tech support!

Another aspect of building a support system that I really encourage as a coach is this: Don't try to reinvent the wheel. If I am confronted with a challenge and I haven't been able to figure out the next step, I ask myself, "Who do I know who could do this really well?" Then I go talk to them and ask for their expertise. The point here is that you don't have to have all the answers and you don't need to fix everything

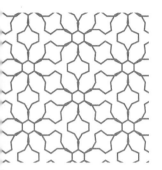

Whenever you need assistance with anything, your first line of defense should be your own community.

yourself. I share this concept with my husband all the time and it really comes in handy when we're running our business.

A few years ago Marc said, "Let's start a line of Hill Country products!" We could have tried to develop the product line and design the packaging on our own. Immediately, I suggested, "Let's go find someone who specializes in product lines, visual marketing, and retail—that will be so much more efficient." I remembered that I knew someone from college who is super talented, and I contacted him to start a conversation. He's been working on the project with us for months now, and it's been an awesome collaboration. In retrospect, having someone help us with the project was the obvious choice; sometimes we just need to remind ourselves that there are so many lovely connections out there and in our personal histories that can make it work.

Whenever you need assistance with anything, your first line of defense should be your own community: It's the best resource there is. Reaching out with a text or email to neighbors and friends where you live and work is the best place to start finding the help you need,

and you might be surprised at how happy people are to be asked. Asking for help and giving it is a two-way street and everybody wins. For example, I am especially grateful for HeyMama, a website community of female professionals and entrepreneurs that I go to on a regular basis and who are always available and willing to help.

So, how does this practice of doing what works actually manifest itself in everyday life? Let's apply it to families for a moment. If you have a child who doesn't love to read—a common struggle for many parents—think about what that child does love to do. Many children love music and can memorize and repeat lyrics all day long. My middle daughter is one of those kids and is actually learning to read while she sings along in endless karaoke sessions. As she sings song after song after song, she's developing a new and high-level vocabulary along the way. Win-win! For children who are more drawn to athletics, sports can help them develop focus and commitment skills—not to mention teamwork, discipline, and playing by the rules—all values that are vital in the classroom (and life). The key is to pay attention to your children's strengths and highlight them.

When I was in school, one thing I was lucky enough to learn was that I could trust my instincts, and I have done that ever since. Whatever decisions I make now are based on that trust, and I'm often quick to shoot from my gut. However, I share my life with a thoughtful partner who is more methodical in his choices, and because of this, I have learned to balance my process and weigh options more before making decisions. Still, when I trust my instincts, they are usually spot-on. Trusting my gut is a crucial mechanism in my decision-making process that saves me time, effort, and energy—it is embedded in my survival DNA.

Of course, instincts lie deep within all of us. Starting with our bodies, they tell us much of what we need to know, sending often subtle but powerful signals. It is the practice of learning to listen to them that spreads this power throughout our experience. We instinctively sense danger; we get apprehensive about walking into one dark parking lot over another; we keep thinking about someone and then they call. Whether it's the hair standing up on your neck, or a little voice saying, "That's not a good idea," our instinct is trying to get our attention. It is always there, trying to reach us—we just need to tune in to it and really listen.

You can work on trusting your instincts just like you target certain muscles when you work out. If you're the type of person who labors over a decision—like my husband, who can take months to decide on a matter because he's so incredibly thoughtful—try taking some quick and easy low- to medium-level risks. Limit your choices and put a timeline on the decision, paying attention to your thought process. Soon, this approach will help you to make choices faster—good time management does so much to reduce our stress—and each time, you'll gain more confidence. The next time you want a contractor to make improvements in your home, for example, meet with two instead of

You can work on trusting your instincts just like you target certain muscles when you work out.

spending half your day interviewing every contractor you can find. You'll end up liking one more than the other and you won't know exactly why—you'll just get a feeling that one of those two individuals will do a better job than the other. I've learned to listen to those instincts and trust the thoughts and feelings they stir, and I encourage you to do the same. When you learn to trust your instincts, you'll be able to recognize more easily what works for you.

THINKWORK

- What in your life is really working right now? How do you know? Describe the feeling and the flow.
- What's not working? Describe the stress and frustration. Did you sense this coming? Were there any red flags that you've been ignoring?
- How can you do what works as it relates to this challenging circumstance? What do your instincts tell you?

5

LIFE LESSON

TRADITIONS: HONOR THEM, CREATE THEM, KEEP THEM

TRADITIONS CELEBRATE OUR PERSONAL NARRATIVE. Everyone wants to feel a sense of purpose, connection, and belonging. Traditions create the framework for our stories, like the chapters in a book. If you come from a family that emphasizes tradition, you already know the feeling of how the history woven in fuels our identity. If you haven't had a lot of traditions in your life, try starting some—or at least just one—and see how it makes you feel. Even if you have inherited traditions, create some of your own—we all need to write our own story, too. You'll find that bringing traditions into your life will attract other like-minded people and build a lot of positive energy—and it's easy and very rewarding.

Traditions ground us and give us something to look forward to, whether it's weekly, monthly, or annually. For example, my family always looks forward to our Fourth of July celebration. We also look forward to Santa Claus stopping by on Christmas Eve, with all of us chanting "SAN-TA! SAN-TA!" That was a tradition in my home when I was growing up, and I remember each year clearly and with such fondness. Now I'm overjoyed that we have brought this cherished tradition to my own little ones. Even our teenagers and college-age cousins still love it! We celebrate our Jewish traditions as well, including Friday night Shabbat (the Sabbath eve) and our annual breaking the fast after Yom Kippur (my kugel skills have gotten quite good!). When I really think about it, I don't just like tradition, I LOVE it!

Some research studies show that children raised with traditions are more confident and secure. They have fewer doubts and less angst knowing there are certain things they can count on, and I really believe this. While my family has been stuck at home during the Covid-19 lockdown, I established a new tradition: the Shelter in Place Dinner. I wanted the kids to feel grounded by a nightly dinner that I served like

clockwork at 7 p.m. every day. This ritual gave us sustenance—literally and emotionally—and helped keep us all tied together.

My kids can always count on having a special breakfast with strawberries and cream every year on Valentine's Day (my favorite holiday), and we drink fruit punch served in champagne flutes (for my son, I substitute his favorite red Gatorade). The day is always filled with lots of love and chocolate. And traditions don't need to be tied to a holiday. Like many couples, one of our most favorite and cherished traditions is Date Night. While that can be a difficult one to uphold in busy lives, Marc and I have kept it going every Thursday evening for the last fifteen years, and it continues to this day.

The traditions around food are not just an anchor for festivity. In times of unrest and great stress, seeking comfort in joining around the table is a common thread among us humans. Most recently, as we all had to hunker down and socially distance ourselves, many of us turned to our tried-and-true favorites, the foods that made us feel good and safe. Americans reported gaining weight, and cookbook sales surged as more and more people expanded their kitchen skills or were cooking for the first time. Social media has become a platform for posting about food and cooking, driven by the tradition of sharing food as a way to nurture yourself and your loved ones both in times of joy and times of need. Whether you enjoy a meal on your own or cook up a feast for family and friends, food lovingly prepared is a panacea for us all. And that's how traditions are started and perpetuated.

Traditions we celebrate at home are still my favorite. I remember the irresistible flavors of Sunday meals in my beloved Italian grandma's very traditional kitchen: roast chicken, homemade pesto, stuffed artichokes, and angel food cake. And no matter what was on the menu, the key ingredient of any meal there was the awesome aura of celebration. Holidays, birthdays, and just plain Sundays all had the same festive flavor that made any time spent with Grandma Millie and Grandpa Giggy so unforgettable. I will always be grateful for those happy days filled with wonderful memories.

Separately from our restaurant lives, an attitude of celebration and ritual in eating together continues to plays a big part in our family: It's the anchor, the glue, that holds us together. Food helps us share who we are—our heritage and culture—with our children in a profound and delightful way. Marc tells the kids stories about his grandparents in Texas and their legendary barbecue gatherings, and I teach them how to layer lasagna the same way my grandma taught me.

On any given day, mealtime allows everyone in our family a moment to pause. Like so many busy people in our culture and others, we're running constantly, kids and adults alike, our minds and bodies perpetually active. When we sit down to a meal and stop thinking about work or school or whatever challenges have taken up our time, it's just the break we need to slow down, connect with each other, and be grateful for our family.

FEASTING ON FAMILY RITUAL

Even before the our nightly Shelter in Place dinners, one of my commitments has been to make and serve a special dinner at home for my family at least once every week. I always set the table with wineglasses, even for the children—filled with water, of course—and before we begin eating, we raise them together in a toast of gratitude for all the wonderful things we are so fortunate to have: We have enough to eat and the love and security of our family. Since we began this little ceremony, it has become one of our most cherished family traditions. Then we are free to enjoy a homemade dinner, which in the summer might include a beautiful quiche with greens, or in winter, the Del Vecchio Family Meatballs over spaghetti (Del Vecchio is my maiden name). I've shared these favorite go-to family recipes here; I encourage you to find some of the recipes of your youth and make them regularly. They will taste wonderful and unearth memories long forgotten.

OUR FAVORITE RECIPES

- Sister Smoothie
- Barbara's Baked Clams
- Summer Quiche
- Del Vecchio Family Meatballs

SISTER SMOOTHIE

Serves 2

My girls Skye, Jaclyn, and especially Geena love smoothies and enjoy making and drinking them for breakfast or lunch, a midday snack, or an on-the-go meal replacer for a quick boost of energy. Our freezer always has a supply of berries and bananas, two key ingredients of this smoothie recipe. We always save any leftover fruit by freezing it and use it in recipes like this one. As many of you know, frozen bananas even taste delicious on their own, like healthy ice cream. On a hot day, just a few bites of frozen fruit make a cool, healthy, refreshing snack. But have fun mixing it up with this smoothie.

- ½ **cup almond milk or milk of your choice**
- 2 **tablespoons honey**
- ½ **banana**
- ¾ **cup frozen blueberries, strawberries, or a mixture or 1 cup fresh berries plus ½ cup ice**
- 1 **teaspoon raw cacao powder or peanut butter (Geena loves this combination).**

In a blender, combine all the ingredients, secure the lid, and purée until smooth. It will be a gorgeous color.

Tip: There are so many options for milk these days. I really like almond milk and my son likes vanilla almond or lactose-free milk. Try cashew milk, oat milk, or coconut water. Of course, whole or low-fat cow's milk is great, too.

BARBARA'S BAKED CLAMS

Makes 30

There are family favorites, and then there is this recipe for my mother's baked clams. These have become legendary with our friends and family. My mom would make these to help celebrate the Feast of the Seven Fishes, a classic Italian tradition on Christmas Eve. The simple but delicious recipe has become a year-round dish to serve whenever the whole family gathers together. My grown nephews, Nick and Craig, can eat a whole tray on their own! I finally convinced my mom to write down her recipe, so now I can share it with all of you. This was no small accomplishment: In our family, nothing is written down, and all great Italian cooks I know cook from memory. My family likes this recipe really garlicky, so feel free to decrease the amount of garlic called for, if you prefer.

- ½ cup chopped fresh parsley
- 2 cups seasoned bread crumbs (my favorite is Progresso brand)
- 6 garlic cloves, finely chopped
- ¾ cup olive oil
- ⅓ cup chicken broth
- 2 (1-pound) containers chopped clams, ⅓ cup of the clam juice reserved
- 30 clamshells
- Cooking spray

1. In a bowl, mix together the chopped parsley, seasoned bread crumbs, and garlic. Add ½ cup of the olive oil and stir with a fork to moisten the bread crumbs, until the mixture is the consistency of wet sand. Add the chicken broth and reserved clam juice and stir to combine.

2. Arrange the clamshells on three baking sheets—10 shells per baking sheet—and spray each individual shell with cooking spray.

3. Spoon about 1 tablespoon of the chopped clams into each shell. Top each with about 1 tablespoon of the bread crumb mixture and gently press it into the clams with a spoon. At this point you can refrigerate the stuffed clams until you're ready to cook.

4. When you're ready to bake, bring the clams back to room temperature and set the oven to broil. Place an oven rack in the middle position of the oven.

5. Drizzle the remaining ¼ cup olive oil evenly over the stuffed clams. Broil for about 5 minutes, or until the tops are golden brown. Be sure to check the oven frequently to make sure they don't burn. Repeat with the remaining baking sheets. Serve immediately.

Tip: You can buy disposable clamshells from the fish market or some supermarkets. If you live near or are visiting the beach when you're planning to make these, you can collect the real thing like my girls often do. Just be sure to wash them carefully before using.

SUMMER QUICHE

Serves 8

Different recipes symbolize different times of the year, and
this delicious quiche reminds me of warm and sunny days,
with people popping over to visit. I bake it in a beautiful
baking dish so I can serve it from the same container, which
makes it even easier to present to guests. For breakfast or
lunch, brunch, happy hour, or even a light dinner with a
fresh baguette and a bottle of wine or sparkling water, this is
one of the most versatile dishes you can make. This quiche
is crustless because I think it's healthier; but you can easily
pour the mixture into a pie shell and bake as instructed.

Olive oil for greasing the baking dish, plus 2 tablespoons

**½ onion, finely chopped (I keep the onions minimal
because my kids don't love them, but this tastes great
with 1 whole onion, or even 2.)**

**2 cups of your favorite greens, or a mix of greens such as
kale, chard, or spinach**

4 large eggs

¼ cup half-and-half

Pinch of salt

Dash of freshly ground black pepper

**½ cup freshly grated cheese such as Gruyère, cheddar, or
Parmesan**

**¼ cup chopped ham or prosciutto, cooked bacon, or
cooked sausage (optional)**

1. Preheat the oven to 350°F. Grease a 9-inch pie pan or similar-sized baking dish with olive oil.
2. Heat 2 tablespoons of olive oil in a large skillet over medium-low heat. Add the onion and sauté until translucent, about 5 minutes.
3. Add the greens to the pan and sauté until they wilt and soften, about 3 minutes.
4. Crack the eggs into a medium bowl. Add the half-and-half and season with the salt and pepper. Whisk until well blended, about 1 minute.
5. Using a wooden spoon, gently fold the greens and onion into the egg mixture. Add the shredded cheese and meat (if using) and gently stir until combined.
6. Pour the mixture into the greased baking dish and bake for 30 minutes, or until the top is set and golden brown. Every oven is different, so start checking at about 20 minutes, to make sure it doesn't burn. Transfer the baking dish to a wire rack and let cool. Serve warm or at room temperature.

Tip: Usually, I leave the quiche out at room temperature for as long as 2 hours during a party because the flavors are best that way, and I know people are going to keep wanting more. If you happen to have any left over, cover the quiche with foil or plastic wrap and refrigerate for up to 3 days. Warm the leftovers gently in a low oven for a nice breakfast treat.

DEL VECCHIO FAMILY MEATBALLS

Serves 4 (but I often double the recipe!)

I love making spaghetti and meatballs. My maiden name is Del Vecchio, and this recipe has been a go-to favorite of my family's for years. My girls and I make them all the time. This version is such a simple combination of ingredients, you'll soon know it by heart—then riff on your own variations! Some members of our family like their meatballs big—about the size of a tennis ball— while others prefer them on the small side, about the size of a large green olive. Just remember to adjust the cooking time depending on how big you make them.

- 1 (24-ounce) jar marinara sauce (I like Rao's brand)
- 1 pound ground "meatball mix" or any combination of ground beef, ground pork, and ground veal
- 1 large egg
- ½ cup freshly grated Parmesan cheese, plus more for serving
- ½ cup plain or seasoned bread crumbs (Progresso is a great shortcut)
- 1 teaspoon chopped fresh garlic
- 3 tablespoons finely chopped fresh parsley
- 3 tablespoons olive oil
- Fresh cooked spaghetti or Italian rolls, split, for serving

1. In a saucepan over medium heat, bring the marinara sauce to a low boil. Reduce the heat to very low and let simmer gently.

2. In a large bowl, using your hands, mix together the meat, egg, Parmesan, bread crumbs, garlic, and parsley until evenly combined. Do not overmix or the meatballs will be tough.

3. Again, using your hands, shape the mixture into balls, sizing them pretty much as large or as small as you like. I usually make mine about the size of a golf ball. Just be careful to adjust the cooking time if yours are bigger or smaller.

4. Heat the olive oil in a large skillet over medium heat. Add the meatballs, taking care not to crowd the pan. You may need to cook them in batches. Cook, shaking the pan occasionally to make sure the meatballs brown on all sides, about 12 minutes total. Using a slotted spoon, transfer the meatballs to a plate.

5. Raise the heat under the marinara sauce to medium and cook until slightly thickened, 8 to 10 minutes. Reduce the heat to medium-low, gently place the meatballs in the sauce, and simmer, turning occasionally, until the meatballs are cooked through, another 10 minutes.

6. Serve hot over spaghetti or in Italian rolls for a meatball sandwich, with plenty of Parmesan.

NAME YOUR FAVORITE TRADITIONS

List your favorite traditions. These are some of mine.

1. Celebrate your birthday—on the day, not before or after.
2. Make the celebration even bigger for milestone birthday years—5, 10, 15, 20.
3. Create a Date Night ritual.
4. Prepare everyone's favorite traditional foods for the holidays together— as a family.

Traditions are also a wonderful part of the fabric of all kinds of relationships, and being the person to drive the creation and perpetuation of them can be very rewarding. At the office, for example, a simple ritual can do much to enrich the workplace experience and celebrate the mini culture of a small group of people. Not only does it make time and space to connect with your coworkers apart from work duties, sharing traditions can help your own performance, the performance of others, and the success of the company. Just take the plunge: Pick any day, week, or month to start a new tradition, and if you need inspiration, Instagram hashtags will always provide. #HappyHour, for example, is an easy, familiar social tradition for bringing people in a workplace together before they run out the door at the end of the day—even those who don't drink, because it's not about alcohol, it's about having a good time, downtime, together, in person or remotely.

HOSPITALITY AT HOME

As an adult, I have always been very professionally
driven. College was, and career is, a top priority
for me. Yet I always had a longer-term vision of
myself surrounded by a big family, preparing
amazing food and presiding over a beautifully set
table. I'm certain that's because I come from a
family of wonderful homemakers, including my
beloved grandmother. Looking at my life now, I
do indeed spend a substantial amount of time in
my kitchen, prepping nightly dinners for six or
more, and it's just another part of our busy life—a
joyous part. The desire to establish traditions
like this has crossed over to the work I do at our
restaurants as I help coordinate the many events
for groups we host, small and large. Today I can
see how I manifested that delicious vision, and
how every decision I made actually moved me to
where I am now. An atmosphere of celebration
is definitely a big part of the Hill Country
experience, and my Community Ambassador
duties at the restaurant are particularly gratifying
to me.

Take a look at your wider circles of family, friends, and coworkers. What kind of traditions would you like to start that will help you connect and align with your goals? I encourage you to think outside the box. You could start a monthly "take your coworker to lunch" day. Or you could set aside a special day to spend with one of your kids—a day in which that one child will get all of your attention (of course, if you have more than one, make sure you set up similar days with them all). You could start a "call my sibling day" and have an actual conversation with your brother(s) and/or sister(s) instead of trying to catch up with them on the fly via email or random text messages. (This idea works for aunts, uncles, grandparents, godparents, and BFF's too!) It's these kinds of traditions that keep loved ones close to you, and you will value the contribution beloved customs make to these relationships for your entire life.

ON THE DAY YOU WERE BORN

Traditions big and small go well beyond the holidays. A perennially partial date to mark is one's birthday . . . our own and our loved ones'. In our house, we always make birthdays a big deal. I am adamant and unapologetically enthusiastic about my commitment to celebrating on the actual day, not before or after—and no exceptions. I think it shows the importance we place on our family members' individual feelings when we make sure to commemorate their important days. Of course that means we sometimes have to get creative. If a kid's

DOUBLY SPECIAL

The opening night celebration for our first restaurant, Hill Country Barbecue Market, was on June 1, 2007, and it was an evening of sizzling music and meat (or, as we like to say, rhythm and 'cue). It was also the night our first child was born. We named our son after the capital of Texas, and Austin arrived on the scene ready to party. On that day every year since, we've had a dual celebration of our two firstborns: our son and our hospitality business. And that same spirit of tradition has set the tone for the birthdays of our three daughters as well.

PLANNING FOR A STELLAR BIRTHDAY CELEBRATION

Ask your children (or kids of all ages) these questions:

- Do you want there to be a theme?
- Do you like decorations and balloons? What kind?
- What is your favorite kind of birthday cake?
- Do you want to celebrate at home or somewhere else?
- Who do you want at the celebration?
- Do you already have some ideas, or do you want to look online for inspiration?

birthday falls on a Tuesday, for example, a sleepover is out of the question. This actually helps kids appreciate the power of planning and thinking ahead while also honoring the significance of that day. For us, with four kids and a very busy work life, this practice makes a lot of sense. When thinking about celebrations, always take the time to figure out what's best for the situation for everyone in your family or family of friends. Remember Lesson 4: do what works.

Keep in mind—especially if you're someone who doesn't like their birthday or are trying to help a loved one embrace theirs—a truly memorable birthday celebration doesn't have to be big or expensive: The keys are to listen, create a wish list, and plan in advance. With our kids, for example, what makes their special days really special is that the event spurs conversations with them about their feelings

Traditions remind us of how wonderful life is.

and desires. It's an opportunity for us to capture where they are in that moment in their lives and maintain our connection and closeness.

Birthday planning, which can be complicated or fraught, is a great example of how to use the Think It, Write It, Share It tools (see page 20)—if we make ourselves break down something we want in our heads, think it through and clarify it, then put it in writing and talk to others about it, we can make it happen with all the positives in place. Party planning, which can seem like a simple thing, is actually a challenging and nuanced process that helps us, and children too, to visualize and manifest—both incredibly useful life skills analogous to setting goals and achieving them. And as a life coach, I see the big picture: observance of traditions is a discipline, and it takes work to keep them alive. It's so worth it to observe them faithfully, because on the most core level, traditions remind us of how wonderful life is.

CELEBRATE SPECIAL TIMES

Special time—a simple and lovely concept as well as a phrase central to Jane Nelsen's education program for adults working with children, detailed in her book *Positive Discipline*—doesn't require extravagant gifts or airplane tickets. Small celebrations or tributes are so often

THINGS TO CELEBRATE THAT AREN'T BIRTHDAYS

- A job well done
- Academic transitions and well-earned grades
- A new home or relocation
- Celebrating the season
- Hosting friends from out of town
- An athletic achievement
- A big promotion

easier to execute than we think, and that can be so helpful, freeing, and motivating to remember. Recognition of an event or milestone (often anything other than major holidays and big days like birthdays get overlooked) makes both kids and adults feel valued and loved. "Special time" can be as simple as taking one hour of your day to take your child out for ice cream, just the two of you. Or meeting your significant other for lunch, when you don't usually have time for that. And here's the trick: It's great if you can plan these special moments ahead of time, but they can be just as special done unexpectedly, on the fly. Spontaneity gets a lot of great press; if you find the opening, go with it, trust that it's worth it. Do it! Maybe after your child's dentist appointment, you stop to play in the park or go to the library. If you are stuck in traffic with them, invent a

AUSTIN'S NIGHT

Teenage boys aren't always eager to spill things to their moms (fellow parents, can you feel me?) I find that if I make special time with my son, it gives him the space to be more open with me; I'll hear about who he's getting along with (or not) at school, or I'll find out about something that upset him (for instance, I didn't know when he was concerned that Dad was working late several nights in a row, until he asked about how our business was doing). Austin and I have carved out two blocks of time together: Either we'll wait until his younger sisters are in bed so we can share a late-night talk, often while watching a ball game at the same time, or I'll take him out for dinner; he gets to choose the spot. If we go out to eat, when we are finished eating, I always ask Austin to guess the bill—a tradition my father started—so he can appreciate the value of his meal. Like his mom, he's gotten quite good at this, and he's usually never more than a few dollars off from the correct amount.

MAKE TIME FOR DATE NIGHT

If you're finally alone with your partner after too much time apart, or are looking to create some special time together after spending too much ordinary time together, and you don't know where to start, ask each other questions: It's a space where you and your partner can connect in a new and positive way, put aside the everyday routines, and connect as partners.

THREE DATE-NIGHT QUESTIONS

- What happened this week?
- How can I help?
- How can we do better together?

new game that only the two of you play.

Start practicing the art of making special time special by planning a couple of mini events. Maybe a picnic to celebrate a child's well-deserved and hard-earned grade or a friend's promotion. And be open to spontaneous celebrations, too. Who knows, that impulse to go see a movie with your best friend to treat her after she finds a new apartment might turn into a more formal tradition of getting together when things happen, which will help ensure that you keep in touch and stay friends for a lifetime.

Special time can be much tougher for couples to carve out, yet it's so important. As many couples will say, we are pretty much stretched to the max all

THINKWORK

- What are your favorite traditions? Which ones do you honor the most?
- Why are they significant or special to you?
- How can you share them with the people who are important to you?
- Where would you like to create a new tradition? Why? How will it positively impact your family?
- Write a few sentences about what this new tradition would look like. What time of year would it take place? Where would it happen?
- Add any details that will make it feel real and help it come to life.

the time with the demands of work, home, and family. So I think, and agree with many others out there, that it's absolutely critical you spend time alone with your partner regularly. Call it whatever you want—we go with old-fashioned "Date Night." This special time is so valuable: It's when the two of you make sure you have dedicated time to connect, communicate, and, hopefully, lay any groundwork needed for positive change! Together, you are creating a safe space to listen and share.

6

IF IT'S NOT RIGHT, GO LEFT

I SAY THIS A LOT TO MY CLIENTS, AND THOUGH IT MAY sound obvious, I am really serious about being open to changing course. If things aren't going right in your life, it's probably time to go left—that is, move yourself away from what's not working. It's what I call "living directionally" (more on this in Lesson 11), and that means being pragmatic and getting clear on knowing exactly where you want to go.

We know that focusing on what works makes us happier people. We've already discussed doing that in Lesson 4. So, what do you do when something doesn't work?

It takes courage and practice to strengthen that risk-taking muscle.

The quick answer is: Stop doing it. Or, if more subtlety is called for: Do it in a different way. This understanding of when to put on the brakes and turn is a vital skill to have. It's scary to change course and follow a different path. It takes courage and practice to strengthen that risk-taking muscle. For starters, keep in mind that it can be any degree of turn: You might need to take a slight left to avoid an obstacle or make a 90-degree turn to try something completely new. Whatever it may be, stay open and commit to changing your course, even if only temporarily. And always ask the question, "Am I moving toward my goal or away from it?" If everything is working for you, enjoy the ride! If not, I promise, taking an alternate route will go a long way to helping you reach your goals.

What if you're lost and just don't know which way to turn? That's when you ask for help, from friends or family or any number of professionals. Consult with your support system and they will help you, either with the answers you are seeking or the tools you need to find your own solution. Remember, you don't need to solve everything yourself.

Your road will not always be straight. There will always be twists and turns. The important thing is to know when to stop, reflect, and

WHEN TO PIVOT

The first job I had after graduating college was one that had me doing exactly what I was meant to do: working for a motivational speaker, developing content on how to drive business. I was right on track. Then I went to a different company that was not aligned with my career goals. This post was a great financial opportunity, so I did what a lot of people do: I prioritized the salary over my professional vision. Although I was successful, I was not happy; nevertheless, I got stuck there for a long while. It took me years to realize that I was no longer headed in the direction I wanted to go. Gradually, as I learned to embrace change, I was able to pivot, turn left, and move back toward my motivational aspirations.

SUCCESS IS
RARELY AN
ACCIDENT.

ask yourself, "Do I know where I'm going?" and "Am I moving toward what I want?" Every lesson in this book will assist you in answering these questions honestly.

One of my favorite personal mantras—which I use all the time in my coaching practice—is, "Success is rarely an accident." I believe that success is achieved when we deliberately and consciously move toward what we want. And no one gets there without a wrong turn or two. That is why we have to know how to move forward and learn to reroute by making different choices next time. I always tell my children, "Mistakes are opportunities to learn" (another *Positive Discipline* tool—thanks again, Jane Nelsen), whether they've made an unfortunate choice or steered themselves into a dead end. It's all okay—that's part of the journey.

Of course, many of us have gotten into the habit of relying on our internal autopilots, much like we rely on the GPS on our smartphones to navigate through unfamiliar terrain. And likewise, we've all driven through areas where the GPS simply doesn't function; all it can do is say, "Rerouting . . ." When that happens, it's up to us to find our own way. And there is no need to panic. There is always a way to figure out how to get where you want to go. Maybe you'll consult a map, or perhaps you'll stop at a gas station and ask someone for directions. In the most basic form, these are ways of "going left": finding a different way to reach your goal. Trust that the directions are within you.

What if things are more complicated—a big area for what we are addressing here—what if, for example, you're really not sure if you are going in a positive direction? When that question or dilemma hits me (and it does, I promise you!), I like to use the More of/Less of tool. It's very simple: On a sheet of paper, write down what you need more of on one side, and what you need less of on the other. It's very similar to a list of pros and cons, and is similarly useful for clearing the view to guide your direction. For instance, if you have a choice between two opportunities and you're split between which one to pick, have the conversation with yourself on what you really want (see page 22). Maybe you want more free time, more creativity, more flexibility, and/or fewer meetings, less commuting time, less supervision, fewer weekend and late-night work hours.

Once you see in writing the things that are important to you, you can start to make choices to move yourself in that direction. Nothing needs to change all at once. Big changes are heavy, so break them down into small changes and make them happen, one or two at a time; they will seem more manageable.

Often, when we look at our children and envision their future, we want them to be what we think will make them secure: a doctor or lawyer, a CEO or banker. I like to remind myself that my kids are who they are, with things that they're good at, things they love to do—and things they can't stand doing. We often look at ourselves this way, too: We may insist on dictating our direction based on what we think we should be doing instead of what we actually want to be doing, sometimes for years at a time. And many people continue on the wrong-for-them path, sometimes for decades, because of status or because the pay is good or because their partner wants them to or for any number of reasons that become blurry or buried. One of my clients stayed in an unfulfilling marriage for seventeen years; she was afraid of the unknown and she didn't know where to turn. She admits now that she wished she'd changed direction much sooner, and I know we can all relate to the comfort zone of sticking with the familiar.

Change can be paralyzing and very frightening; however, we have to remember the truth in the saying: It is never too late to make a change. I truly understand, because I've been there, too. I was in an on-and-off relationship for several years before tying the knot for the first time. Then, after just one year of marriage, it became very obvious that we were not good for each other. The relationship became dysfunctional and I grew increasingly unhappy. I knew something wasn't working, so I had a difficult decision to make: I could stick with it, as my traditional values dictated, or I could go left and see what a different path had to offer. It took me a while. Eventually I chose to change my course, even though it led me through some very tough times. I knew it was a positive decision, even during my time on an uncertain path before it led me to where I am today.

Part of turning left includes what you do and how you do it. Maybe you think you don't like biking—because you've never tried a scenic bike tour. Or perhaps you hate cooking—maybe because you've always done it alone. What if you and your partner or a friend made plans to cook together? That might turn an experience into something to enjoy rather than avoid. The same goes for exercising, cleaning house, or spending time with relatives—any activity you try to avoid or that you might find unpleasant. Take a look at the negative things in your life. Examine them one by one. How many of them can you turn into a "possible positive"? I challenge you to make a left-hand turn and direct yourself toward what you really want.

WHAT'S WORKING?

Okay, I just want to take a moment here. Although we've been talking for over half a book now about things like embracing change, establishing traditions, what to do when something is not working—I want to say that it's also important to constantly remind yourself of what is working. Take a step back and acknowledge at least one thing in your life that is going well—those are powerful Life Lessons in

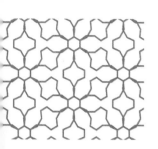

I challenge you to make a left-hand turn and direct yourself toward what you really want.

THE WRITE THING

Believe it or not, dear reader, here's something I have never liked: writing. I love sharing with others and I love writing in my personal journal—I've got literally hundreds of notebooks filled with entries to prove it, dating all the way back to my school days. Still, what do I find super intimidating? Writing things for large numbers of people to read—a blog posting, a magazine article, or (yikes!) a book. These were all things I would procrastinate on or simply avoid doing at all—largely because my dyslexia would cause me embarrassment (read my Instagram feed and you'll "no" what I mean).

So, I changed my course. If I couldn't write well myself, I would look for someone to help me. (Use your support system!) I found a wonderful collaborator who not only helps me improve my message, she has helped me find my written voice. When we work together, she makes sure that everything I write is the Best Version (page 20) it can be. Working with her has been a gift and has changed my whole outlook on writing. With her help, I feel so much more confident in sharing my written words.

THINKWORK

- List three things in your life that are going well—where you are in flow and really satisfied.
- Is there something in your life that obviously isn't working?
- How could you "go left" and do it differently?
- Can you use this positive energy to help motivate additional change?

themselves. It's very easy to feel bogged down in the negative when you start identifying what is wrong or off, so I want to be very clear that it's important to keep your eye on the positive too. BUT it's even more important to move away from what's not working to allow yourself to really create the space for the good. It's a dance of balance, using the information in your heart. While no one can be on their mark 100 percent of the time, the goal should always be to stay positive, celebrate what's working, and move forward toward your ultimate desire. This will give you a feeling of confidence and renewed energy, and will continue to motivate and inspire you to eliminate anything that's not working.

LOVE IS A CHOICE

WE'RE OFTEN LED TO BELIEVE THAT LOVE IS fated—that the partner you're meant to be with is pre-arranged by some unseen force that's bigger than us. While that's a very romantic idea, and the stuff that fairy tales and movies are made of, I see love differently—and I'm a hardcore romantic. I've always been endlessly in love with love. My theme song might as well be "Addicted to Love," because I truly believe that love is the ultimate high. I also believe that love doesn't choose us: We choose it—or we don't.

Love is a choice: and yours to make. I've always been a big fan of partnership and collaboration. I don't do much by myself—not even writing this book—so for me, happiness is not going to be possible by flying solo in my personal life. Even as a child, I always knew I'd grow up to be one half of a married couple. As early as kindergarten, I was writing down the names of the boys on my school bus and creating a rotating schedule to sit with each one of them. I would purposely play hide-and-seek with boys to find dark, cramped spaces. Yes: I was playing the field at age seven! My parents were my early role models. They were high school sweethearts, and they've been married for over fifty years. From their example, I always believed that marriage was forever. Even today, Valentine's Day is my absolute favorite holiday. (If my kids are reading this right now, they're laughing.)

What if we make a choice in the arena of romance and it turns out to be the wrong choice? Of course, we've all been there, some of us many times. Then, if we're lucky, there comes a time when everything points to, this is it, "the one." And yet, it isn't. The feeling is creeping up on you, but you really don't want to admit it—not this time! This is the moment to dig in with the Life Lesson tools. As fated as a romance may feel, it is still a choice. If your instincts are telling you you've made the wrong choice, listen, and ask yourself: Is this relationship moving me in the direction of my goals, or the opposite? If it's moving you away, what are you going to do about it?

MAKING MISTAKES

After college, I was away on business in Washington, D.C., and staying at a friend's apartment. Her roommate was away for the weekend, so I stayed in his room. There, I saw photographs of a tall and lean blond guy with a big smile. Interesting books were stacked on the shelf, including literature on business and travel and cigars; the bed was draped with a cashmere blanket. I found myself falling in love with this guy before even meeting him; I could hardly wait for him to get home.

Of course, it wasn't real. I knew that much even then. Just the same, I was intent on meeting the occupant of the room I was staying in—so much so that I didn't go to the training center for work, which was my reason for being in D.C. in the first place. Instead, I stayed in the room, waiting for my crush to get home. My friend tried warning me: "You don't want to meet him," she said. I was filled with confidence and ignored her.

He finally arrived, and was so charismatic that he had me at "Hello." The fireworks were like the Fourth of July. I couldn't keep my head on straight. I called my mom to tell her I'd met the man I was going to marry. I did not do the work of finding out who he was and what he was really like. I was infatuated, and I dove in without testing the water's depth. A short time later we were engaged.

Within six months, my fiancé wasn't coming home at night; sometimes he would disappear for a day or two at a time. Unfortunately, he turned out to be a party boy, irresistibly attracted to alcohol and substance abuse. It was really hard. He refused therapy. I married him anyway. Just one year after the wedding, I found myself not just depressed about my relationship, but also without direction, for my career, my dreams, my identity. I had to admit to myself that I was not making decisions that were moving me in a positive direction; I was not living directionally (although I wasn't calling it that back then yet; see Life Lesson 11!). Still, I loved my husband—and wasn't love supposed to last forever?

I'd always envisioned myself having a big family, and here I was: married, and really questioning whether I could have children with a partner like this.

By my thirtieth birthday, I was completely miserable. I remember being with him at a nightclub. It was two o'clock in the morning and I was in the ladies' bathroom, looking at myself in the mirror. All I could think was, "Where are you going?" I didn't recognize the person looking back at me.

Finally, I convinced my husband to see a couples' therapist, who spoke to us together, and then asked to speak to me alone. "If you choose to be with this man, you have to know that your life will be filled with empty promises, disappointments, and disappearing acts." I had to acknowledge that I had made a poor choice by marrying a person who was wrong for me. And maybe I was also wrong for him.

The unraveling of that partnership was especially difficult for me because of my lifelong infatuation with love and my cherished belief that marriage was supposed to last a lifetime. Although I knew I was doing the healthy thing in separating from my spouse, it felt like an epic failure in my eyes.

When I chose not to settle for less than everything I had always envisioned, however, my failure translated into an epic win: Now that I was seeing things more clearly, I was available and open, and that's how and why I met the wonderful man who is now my husband.

I could have given up on the hope for the love I'd always dreamed about. Instead, I made a choice: Hit the do-over button and don't look back. And while it may sound too simple, or callous, to do that, I had to set aside fear, embrace change, and choose to find the love I wanted, no matter how hard that was going to be.

When you commit to living your Best Version (see page 20), you'll find that all aspects of your life begin to align, and you will notice that you're in flow—you know, you're in the zone!—and people will take notice. When everything is in sync in your life, you will naturally become more attractive to the people you want to meet.

Why this is so important is, it makes you ready for the right love— even if it comes in a form you weren't expecting. My husband, Marc, is quite different from what I'd imagined the love of my life would be, and yet he's everything I could have wanted. We have an honest, authentic partnership, he's loyal and supportive . . . and he always comes home at night.

Of course, even the perfect relationship is imperfect. When you love a person and things become difficult, as they always will at times in any relationship, remind yourself then too that love is a choice: Focus on all the reasons you chose this person when you first fell in love. "I adore my partner. I think he/she is smart, kind, honest, and that is why I chose to love him/her." Remember the positive attributes that moved you toward this person, and why you committed to your relationship. Remember that liking your partner is the first step to loving your partner. Ask yourself if you really like them. If the answer is yes, you then choose to work with them to overcome any obstacle.

Choosing to leave a relationship is incredibly hard. It's never a first option, and if it does come to that point when you realize that your paths are no longer going in the same direction—that's okay.

And it's not all about you. Splitting up may help both of you find the loving partners you want, and that will fulfill your lives.

I must admit, for all the help and motivation I try to give others every day, sometimes I get very low and depressed, even angry and out of sorts. Fortunately, those feelings only come out for a few hours at any given time, and a lot of people who know me have never seen them. But my partner certainly has! And this is what I'm talking about when I talk about love being a choice: Your partner knows what you are like when you are at your best, and they know you at your worst. No one is perfect. Marc knows that about me all too well. When you choose to love someone, you must choose to love everything about them, even when they aren't at their best.

THINKWORK

- Make a list of the characteristics or traits you would love to have in a partner.
- Check back on this list when you meet someone and see how they measure up.
- If you are married, list all the reasons you chose this person. Refer to this list when things are challenging.
- How can you really show up for your partner this month and choose love with your whole heart?

8

STAY IN YOUR LANE

I SHAPED THE LESSONS IN THIS BOOK SO THEY WOULD all work together, to help us to move in a positive direction. Staying in your lane is about staying the course as you follow the goal of being your authentic self. It's integral to my coaching philosophy, practice, and personal and professional life.

The concept may sound simple, yet it's actually quite complicated. I confess, it's one I need to revisit regularly myself. Clients have asked

Focus on yourself—your own goals—and avoid getting sidetracked by the goals of others.

me whether staying in your lane means limiting yourself somehow or boxing yourself in. I say no. Staying in your lane allows you the freedom to focus—really focus—on yourself. It's a commitment to growth, to forward motion, and positive progress without the distraction of comparison. Creating mindful goals and moving toward them is key, and the idea of staying in your lane adds a visual understanding, leading to a belief in yourself. This concept ultimately gives you the strength and confidence to support your career and your home life. It's like you are driving a car on a multilane highway. If you want to be a conscientious driver, you need to shift your focus constantly to watch the road and to keep an eye out for hazards. If you lose your concentration, you could swerve and crash. It's critical not to get distracted by whatever is next to you—there may be a lot of traffic and noise, and if you look around too much, you can become distracted and begin to drive off course.

In life, there will always be something to distract you: the shiny Lamborghini that you know you'll never have (unless that's your goal, of course) or someone's apparently perfect life on Instagram that seems so much better than your own.

Remember: Your goals matter.

When I suggest you stay in your lane, I'm encouraging you to focus on yourself—your own goals—and avoid getting sidetracked by the goals of others. Don't let other people get in your head: Let them stay in their lane and you stay in yours. They have their goals, you have yours. The two do not need to cross. It sounds like a simple rule, yet we break it all the time. Remember: Your goals matter, and they are best achieved when you focus on them. Even if some of your goals seem to align or be similar to someone else's, remember that your goals and your path are truly unique to you. Trying to sync up your goals with another person will only stir up negativity and comparison and steer you away from what you want. While doing this may sound limiting, it's actually wonderfully liberating. Oscar Wilde captured the concept perfectly: "Be yourself; everyone else is already taken."

When you're working toward your Best Version (see page 20) with each of your small and large goals, absolutely nothing should have the power to derail you. Sometimes, of course, this is easier said than done. For example, we've all experienced that discourteous driver who gets pushy and starts to tailgate us, practically attaching their front fender to our rear one. Even in this situation, you have two good choices: Ignore the driver and stay focused, or change lanes briefly and let them go by. In both instances, you can stay focused and continue toward your destination. In life, we shouldn't let anything or anyone force us off the track or away from our goals. We want to be watchful and aware so we can identify if a situation we're in is making us move out of our lane.

I have briefly discussed sharing and the positive aspects of social media, and how Instagram, Twitter, and Facebook can help us commit to our goals. But: You must also be mindful about overdoing it with social media, because even your go-to platforms have their downsides. Keeping tabs on other people's feeds is a major time suck and a wide avenue of distraction. When you allow yourself to become distracted by the progress of others—your competitors, your coworkers, your relatives—you take energy away from your own progress. With social media letting you in on the lives and daily activities of so many people, it's very easy to enter a superhighway of other lanes and forget all about your own.

In life, we shouldn't let anything or anyone force us off the track or away from our goals.

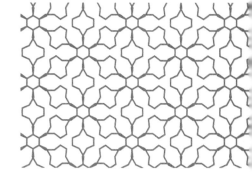

KEEPING IT REAL ON SOCIAL MEDIA

I'll admit it: I've hired photographers to make my Instagram feed look more polished. I know, I know. Just like so many others. For me, almost surely as for them, it was a marketing decision. But if in any way it seems like I was trying to make my life appear perfect, I apologize—or at least, I have to disagree. My life is far from perfect, and that's why you'll see me on my Instagram live stream "Coffee Talk," where I discuss issues and concerns I'm having, at 6.30 a.m., in my bathrobe, with no makeup. I do this because I like to share and communicate, and also because I want you to see me, you who are connected to me in that realm, in real life. My goal is to be my Best Version (page 20) always, and to continue moving toward the person I want to be—and that's why I share myself, share it all with you, without any glossy prep. I want to inspire you to keep doing the work and keep making positive decisions, and you inspire me at the same time. And I want my images to convey a message: one of realness, sincerity, inspiration, possibility, and hope. My hard work has paid off for me, and I believe yours will, too.

Truly, I want to be sure not to oversimplify this lesson. In life, there will always be distractions, and they are real. It can be extremely difficult not to be affected by the people around you—partners, parents, colleagues, children, neighbors—especially if they are carrying negative energy. You want to reach a point of maturity where you don't allow anyone's behavior to significantly impact you. It's the negative energy of other people that sometimes makes it hard to continue on your own path. It can be the ultimate distraction, and it can prevent you from making the positive choices that move you where you want to go. This is one of my biggest challenges: I get really affected by background noise, and therefore I have to work on this on a daily basis to stay on track.

So, what do you do when someone you love throws a fit, says hurtful things, and stomps away? It's always tempting to say hurtful things back and react in kind. And sometimes you will really, really want to. However, if you jump in and react that way, you are using the primitive side of your personality—the part that some psychologists call the

Try to rise above the situation, no matter how unpleasant it may be, and get back to your lane and your goals.

"reptilian brain"—and it's definitely not your Best Version (page 20). Doing this will turn you away from your goal, not toward it. Instead, try to rise above the situation, no matter how unpleasant it may be, and get back to your lane and your goals. Remember, it's a distraction and if you engage, it will take you off track. I still work on this one a lot—my Italian temper does not help matters!

Let me share with you some strategies that have worked for me.

First, try making it not about you. Say something to the effect of, "I'm so sorry you're having such a hard time; I'm here for you whenever you want to reconnect." I use this tactic with my children when they're upset past the point of reason: "I'm here to listen whenever you're ready."

Second, remember losing your temper, whether it's cursing out another driver, a business professional, or even your partner, won't help you reach your goals. Just like road rage, it will slow down your progress even more. Before I pounce on my husband to correct or confront him about an issue, I do my best to connect with him. In *Positive Discipline*, this is called "connection before correction." So, I'll try to stop before I start yelling and say first, "That was really great that you did (insert action here). Now, do you have a few minutes? Can we talk about (insert challenge here)?" For example: "That's really great that you made the family dinner. Can we discuss you leaving the kitchen a mess and who is responsible for cleaning it?" Or, "I think it's terrific that you went ahead and planned a vacation for the family. Can we

talk about the conversation we had about trying to cut back on spending? And that this is moving us away from what we said we wanted, which is to grow our savings?"

Very often, success in a stay in your lane exchange is all about the way you present what's on your mind. It's about being sensitive and putting the other person first, like being a courteous driver: You slow down to let another motorist pass in front of you without giving it a second thought.

At the end of the day, the concept is there to help you stay on course and always move forward. If you take care to stay in your lane, you will realize what is most important to you: your friends, your family, your community, and your contributions to the world. And most important, it helps you enjoy your ride.

THINKWORK

- How does "staying in your lane" apply to you right now?
- What distracts you and makes you lose focus?
- How can you better stay in your lane?
- Why is this important to you? Make a list of the benefits.

LIFE LESSON

STOP
WINE-ING

"**I**'M SO MUCH BETTER WHEN I DRINK!" SAID NO ONE, ever. I have a confession to make: The other evening, I failed to take a page from my own playbook. Want to know how? I had four glasses of wine. Absolutely no one is their Best Version (page 20) when they drink excessively. The truth of the matter is, there's nothing two glasses of wine can't fix—and three glasses won't make worse. Remember, three strikes and you're out.

Don't get me wrong; I'm no teetotaler. What is more romantic than pouring a glass of wine with a nice dinner or downing a cold beer by the pool on a hot day or sipping a margarita on the beach while on vacation?

However, after years of using alcohol for fun, I realized I was also using it to avoid uncomfortable situations or to hide feelings (not to mention starting to see the damage it did to my previous relationships). Now I try to reserve this indulgence for special occasions, the good times. What I've learned above all with alcohol: It's a slippery slope. One or two drinks can relax you; three or four can turn you into a person you don't want to be. I've seen this with myself, and I have also dated alcoholics and recovering alcoholics.

FIVE ALTERNATIVES TO HAVING A COCKTAIL

I think so many of us fell prey to the bottle when the Covid-19 crisis first hit—no wonder liquor stores were deemed "essential." In the end, like every other indulgence, alcohol needs to be kept in check, no

One or two drinks can relax you; three or four can turn you into a person you don't want to be.

KICKING BACK

One day I was visiting a girlfriend's house. She'd set up a game of soccer for our kids, so we kicked back and enjoyed rosé outside on a picnic blanket. It was honestly one of the best summer moments I can remember. The weather was so lovely, the kids were running around, and my friend and I were chitchatting and sipping wine. Then I walked down the road to pick up my daughter from another party, where I had a second glass of wine with a different group of friends. Everything was terrific, and that should have been the end of it: two stops, with a glass of wine at each.

You can see where this is heading. I came home and had another glass of wine . . . and another. Then my husband called, and we went down a rabbit hole of a needless argument. With dismay, I realized that would not have happened had the third glass . . . and the fourth . . . not been poured. Drinking too much wine had turned me into a whining winer. If I had been using my "Begin. Focus. Commit." tool (see page 39), which helps me stick to my goals, I would have been able to keep my alcohol intake in check.

Often, I'll begin my morning by committing to a plan for eating and general health. I'm always careful to keep it positive by choosing the words of my intention carefully. So in this case, instead of, "No alcohol today," I'll say, "I will have two drinks today." (I've never liked the word "No" and most other people don't either. "No" so often feels like punishment.) I remind myself that limiting my alcohol intake to two drinks is my Best Version (page 20). Or, if I'm planning on a dry day, I'll keep it positive by affirming, "Alcohol cleanse today! Yay!" Once the intention is set, I hold myself accountable. By doing this, I can focus on the things that are important to me, which may have been sidetracked if alcohol was involved.

I know that this can be a tough lesson to swallow. I have to do this because I like alcohol, yet I recognize that it does not make me a better person—and being better is my ultimate goal. So I have to monitor my alcohol consumption closely, and I willingly admit that it can be hard. As with any addiction—to cigarettes, or certain kinds of food—I want to go there, even when I know it's not good for me. Today, I have trained myself to wake up each day and remind myself that I'm better alcohol-free because I see my goals more clearly. You can do this, too.

matter what. As so much wisdom before has said, too much of anything isn't good for us. I don't eat chocolate doughnuts every day, and I shouldn't be enjoying cosmopolitans every day, either. "Everything in moderation" may sound like old advice, and I still say it because it's very good advice!

If you've struggled with alcohol, trust me, I feel you. I come from a family that loves drinking. Whenever my dad visits, he walks through the door, greets us all—and what's the first thing he does? Makes martinis. That is our culture, our tradition: We have a festive family!

The trick is not to be overly festive. Over time, I have established a nice balance while still having healthy boundaries. When I head into a party where the spirits are flowing, I'll set a goal that doesn't involve drinking, like committing to introducing myself to at least one new person or learning something new about someone at the party I already know. I often go to fundraisers with my husband. These benefits are both a professional perk and an occupational hazard—and on the way there, I will actively seek support from him by sharing my intention. I'll turn to him and say, "I'm going dry tonight," or I'll say, "I'm only having one because my higher intention is to make a significant connection here tonight."

Whether we know it or not, we're all more thoughtful and engaging without alcohol. To that end, here are the top alternatives to a cocktail I like to share:

1   **Use some elegant stemware as your everyday water glass.**
    Hydration really is essential for good health, and if you love
    to drink like I do, this "everyday elegance" detail will motivate
    you to drink more water. At our family's dinner table, my kids
    really enjoy drinking water from fancy glasses. Often, I'll refill
    my own wineglass with water, whether flat or sparkling: For
    me, what really signals party time is not necessarily what you
    drink, it's what your drink is served in. Festivity is the vessel,
    not the juice. Sparkling water with a twist of lime? Yes, please!
    In a champagne glass.

2   **Make a simple fruit punch or sangria for summer, or mulled
    cider in winter—just omit the alcohol, and double down on
    fresh fruit and fruit juices and/or mulling spices.** Mix up a
    healthy mocktail with simple pantry staples like coconut water
    or pineapple juice . . . anything that conjures the tropics. Or use
    the blender to mix up a healthy Virgin Mary with tomato juice
    and fresh celery—and maybe some fresh ginger, turmeric, and
    black pepper for good measure. And don't forget the garnishes:
    more celery, olives, lemon, jalapenos, horseradish. All good,
    and good for you. (There are many, many delicious mocktail
    recipes online and in cookbooks.)

3   **Try to enjoy three cups of tea a day—and really savor them.**
    For me, in the evening, when family or friends are going for
    an after-dinner drink, I'll have a cup or two of tea. I still can't

believe how much better I feel in the morning when I don't have that sugary sambuca or Grand Marnier hangover. Having tea instead makes a huge difference in how I feel. Bonus if the tea has a wellness benefit, like a simple infusion of fresh ginger (great for the digestion) or brewed chamomile (calming, to promote restful sleep). My absolute favorite wintertime tea is good old Celestial Seasonings Cinnamon Apple Spice.

4 **Write in your journal about skipping alcohol.** Be sure to do this in a positive way that emphasizes the fun and benefits of staying sober. Don't dwell on the missing booze—instead, focus on the plus side of choosing to be alcohol-free. Some people even keep dedicated drinking journals, just like an exercise or diet journal. I like to incorporate my drinking goals into my everyday journal. A sample entry may read, "I am healthier alcohol-free; I am calmer alcohol-free; I am lighter alcohol-free; I am better alcohol-free." I really cheer myself on. I find using repetition in a journal to be very effective in motivating an outcome.

5 **Connect with friends.** If you still feel that festivity is lacking, call a friend to catch up—that's as addictively enjoyable as any spiked drink, especially if your friend lives far away and an in-person get-together is not possible. On a FaceTime call, you can relax and genuinely connect.

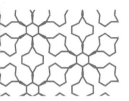

The real key to keeping this commitment is staying positive.

When I do a day without alcohol, I love how great it makes me feel: productive, alert, firing on all cylinders. Try it. If you like to drink, I know it's hard to believe. After just a few days without alcohol, I bet you'll say to yourself, Why can't I feel this way all the time, every day? You can! Instead of having that drink, you could be focusing on your goals. Nothing feels better than the focus of a clear head.

If you want to commit to abstaining from alcohol, hold yourself accountable and don't be afraid to ask someone to help you stay the course. I always share my intention with my husband first, whether or not we're going out to a party.

The real key to keeping this commitment is staying positive. I committed to Dry January two years ago, and I found myself seriously tempted by alcohol many times. My husband and I spend a good deal of our days hosting and attending events where liquor is flowing freely, so there's temptation at every turn. It's often challenging to turn down a drink. So I started focusing on the positive things that going dry would do for my well-being: I'll feel less dehydrated, I'm giving my liver a break, my skin will look brighter, I'll have a better workout tomorrow . . . and in doing so, I reinforce for myself that I

didn't actually want the booze. Another bonus is that the nights I don't consume are nights I teach my children that alcohol isn't necessary for a good time.

These days there are so many wonderful alternatives. My current favorites are Clausthaler Dry-Hopped nonalcoholic beer from Germany; Upside Dawn Nonalcoholic Golden by Athletic Brewing Co., which has breweries in Connecticut and California; Curious Elixirs "booze-free cocktails" from New York's Hudson Valley (their clever slogan? "Shaken, Not Slurred"); and the spicy citrus raw juice blend from New York City's Juice Press. You can put social media to work for you by Instagramming your favorite satisfying drinks, tagging the companies that make them, and sharing them with your friends—like a non-drinking journal. I'm always surprised by how many positive, inspiring comments I have received on Instagram about what I'm not drinking! You'll get instant inspiration from all the comments I am sure you will receive, too. People love not drinking together.

Go easy on yourself. Just because everyone else is observing Dry January doesn't mean that's how you have to do it. January is an especially social month for Marc and me, with a greater-than-usual amount of celebrations going on. So we go dry (or dry-ish) for a different month instead: one year it was November, the next it was December. Who knows, it might just become an annual Glosserman tradition— and you know how I like to observe traditions. Do what works for you.

THINKWORK

- How much did you drink this week? Do you have a healthy relationship with alcohol?
- How can you have a better relationship with alcohol? Set some goals.
- Track your drinks this month. How are you doing?
- List the benefits of drinking less.
- Write down how you feel after not drinking for five days. Do you feel different in your energy and focus?

10

HAPPINESS IS A SERIES OF GOOD DECISIONS

IN THE SONG "HAPPY," BY PHARRELL WILLIAMS, THERE'S a lyric that really resonates with me: "Clap along if you know what happiness is to you." Here's what happiness—true happiness—is to me: a series of good decisions. I don't think success happens by accident. Just like any form of achievement, there is a journey, a series of choices or decisions that get us to the place we want to be. And each of those decisions is made by me—and you. If you make each decision thoughtful and intentional, they will be good ones, and the possibility of happiness will become a reality—your reality.

People look at me all the time and ask, "Why are you so happy? How come you're always smiling?" The truth is, I do smile a lot, and that's because I have a lot to smile about . . . now. It took me a very long time—years and years—to get to this place. Happiness doesn't happen overnight, for anyone. When you make positive, thoughtful decisions, you begin living directionally (see Lesson 11), and happiness will follow. This can take some time and patience, and you will see it approaching in little shifts and changes.

Journaling (see page 13) can really help you with this transition, because as you put words on paper, you will be clarifying your feelings as you document your thoughts. Be open-minded and allow those good things to come. Recognize the little blessings even in the face of difficult times; there is always something good happening, even if it's small, and this will also help you lift your thoughts and feelings into something more positive, more grateful. Developing a positive mindset is another key to your overall happiness and it will set you on the road to achieving your goals.

Happiness always needs to be nurtured—constantly, vigilantly—every single day.

I'm in my happy place today because I made a conscious, 24/7 effort to make good decisions, even when a less-than-good decision could have been made more easily. Happiness will be the outcome for your hard work—the hard work of living directionally and staying the course until you reach your goal. This work is definitely a labor of love, and it never stops. Happiness always needs to be nurtured—constantly, vigilantly—every single day. There's no vacation from this work and no salary, though truly, the benefits are priceless. And when you change your mindset to look for happiness, it will feel less like work and more like a gift. The payoff for investing so much effort and care in living directionally is that you will make happiness possible in your own life, even when it seems totally impossible.

WATCH YOUR WORDS

The words you choose, whether you are writing them down or speaking them out loud, will affect how you feel and direct you toward your ultimate outcome. Remember to choose neutral or positive words. Instead of saying, "I'm a wreck today," try rephrasing it with, "I'm having a challenging day." Being challenged is far more neutral than being a wreck. I once coached a client to eliminate the word "stress" altogether, and she has shared that it's made an incredible positive impact on her life. Always look for the words that will lift you up instead of those that drag you down. It will make a difference, and it's one of those small steps that move you in a positive direction.

As Audrey Hepburn famously said, "Nothing is impossible: The word itself says, 'I'm possible.'"

I always tell my husband, "You are the best decision I ever made." My family life isn't perfect—nobody's is. I try not to complain, because it was my choice and I made the commitment to stand by this choice and follow it all the way through. And that's one reason why our family is happy—because we made what I believe to be a series of good decisions that got us to the goal of a solid partnership and four beautiful children. People often tell me I'm lucky. And some days, yes, I feel like the luckiest person in the world. However, the blessings I have in my life are not just the luck of the draw. I've trained myself to make good decisions. And I hope to help you to do the same.

So, how do we get in the habit of making good decisions? Every single day of our lives, we're faced with thousands of choices, big and small, from what to have for breakfast to where to focus our professional energy. This can be overwhelming, so let's break it down.

You are about to eat pancakes and sausage for breakfast. Before you indulge, ask yourself, "How is this meal serving me? Is it moving me toward or away from my goal of staying healthy?"

This may sound like a silly and simple exercise. Truthfully, I use this method of asking myself throughout the day, and that practice keeps me moving forward. It truly takes only a moment—a simple pause before digging into those pancakes—and your choice will either keep you pointed in the direction of your goal or it will knock you off track.

I once had a client with a tendency to take on a lot of guilt, which caused her to overcommit to things. She was an open communicator, so she would often find herself overextending herself to appease others. I suggested that in those situations, she should pause and ask herself, "Is what I'm offering serving the conversation?" In many cases, the answer was, "No." That would stop her from making commitments she didn't truly want to make. She would also ask herself, "Does this conversation serve me?" This helped her stop oversharing her thoughts, and she no longer felt remorse later for sharing information she knew she should keep to herself. She realized, too, that if a conversation did not serve her, it probably didn't serve anyone else either. After she began asking herself these simple questions, she noticed that her stress level went way down and her happiness went way up.

With each decision you face, you want to prioritize your own happiness. The only person who can decide whether your decisions are making you happy is you.

In my coaching practice, I encourage clients to consider three important things every time they are faced with a decision: Work, Home, and Life. None of these areas can exist completely independently; there is always some crossover. That's why I firmly believe that what we choose to do professionally—our career—must be in sync with what we want our home life to be and what we're passionate about personally.

"NOTHING IS IMPOSSIBLE: THE WORD ITSELF SAYS, 'I'M POSSIBLE.'"

—AUDREY HEPBURN

Let's say you're a devoted parent who wants to spend a lot of time with your children. If that's the case, you may not want a job that puts you in China for three months out of the year. Not because you can't do it, rather because it wouldn't be aligned with what you want domestically. I believe we are happiest when our work and home lives are aligned. For me, that means that when I have to make a decision in one area of my life (work), I need to consider the goals I have for my family (home). The choices you make have to make sense for all the things you want out of life. Always.

Consider how many things you do each week that truly make you happy. If you haven't thought about your life in those terms lately, it's a good question to ask yourself. You can train yourself to make the kind of positive choices that will lead you toward happiness. For example, I'm constantly telling my kids to make choices that make them happy, not me. When the school year starts, I consult each child when they're picking activities outside of mandatory studies for the semester, and I tell them, "Don't choose based on what your siblings or friends are choosing. Choose two that are going to make you happy." Our children have been delighted to learn this lesson, and I see them implementing it in different ways.

One of the reasons I love parenting so much is that it's so obvious when children are happy. When they're happy, they wear a big smile and they can't wait to go out there, for any activity they love. I can't tell you how many conversations I've had with other parents who complain that their kids don't want to do this or that thing. Just like us adults, the thing you do should bring you joy. Why waste time making your kids go to karate if they don't really enjoy martial arts?

Another example: I've always thought a piano would be a nice thing to have in our home. I have asked my children a hundred times, "Who wants to play piano?" And nobody has wanted to yet (I love the word "yet." It creates possibilities. I'm still trying.). Then, on a recent vacation, I tried rallying everyone to head to the tennis courts. It was a beautiful day and I felt like swinging. My son, Austin, was psyched and put on his athletic shorts, while my girls wore frowns. Instead of forcing everyone to play, I let the girls head (very happily) to the playground while Austin and I finished our match (he beat me 6-3). This was a nice reminder to me of one of my own bits of advice: Forcing our kids to do something they don't want to do will not lead to their happiness—or ours.

There are exceptions, of course—for example, doing chores is non-negotiable. When it comes to extracurricular activities, however, if it doesn't bring you or your partner or your kids happiness, it's not something you or they have to do.

And another incentive for not pushing kids to do things that don't interest them? You will save money and time. Things like tennis lessons are pretty pricey, and in our house, the game table gets far more use than a piano ever would—and it takes up about the same space.

Bottom line: It's important to give your kids choices within a specific structure. If my daughter doesn't like tennis, that doesn't mean she can hole up in her room and play video games. I will encourage her to try something else. She knows that she needs to choose another activity that will keep her moving and active.

I am committed to making decisions daily, weekly, and monthly that will make me happy. One thing that has always made me happy is movement. Whether it's dancing or running, I love being in motion. I'm happiest when I'm active. If I don't have quality movement for two weeks, I'm a different person; it's a Jekyll-and-Hyde situation. My husband recognizes it and will say, "You've got to go for a run." He knows how my whole mood changes when I'm not active—and how running instantly uplifts me. Think about what makes you happy, and the things you want to have in your life—again, daily, weekly, and monthly—to continue to lift your spirits and inspire your positive direction. That is what will lead you to your own personal happiness.

THINKWORK

- When was the last time you did something that made you truly happy? What was it? Describe how it made you feel.
- Make a Happy List: Write down five things that always move you in a positive direction. Hang it somewhere you can see it.
- Create a discipline of asking yourself questions. "How is this serving me?" is a good place to start.

11

LIFE LESSON

LIVE DIRECTIONALLY

THINK ABOUT THE LIFE YOU'VE ALWAYS WANTED, down to the smallest detail: the house, the apartment, the street, the car, the career, the office, the desk, the vacations you want to take, the destinations you'd like to visit, the interests you hope to cultivate. Really concentrate, and visualize all of these things. Living directionally is all about vision—it's a method to manifest the lifestyle you want.

LIVING

DIRECTIONALLY

IS ALL ABOUT

VISION.

As I've mentioned more than once, I love to move. Learning new dance steps and routines comes easily to me. Still, there is one dance that I constantly need to practice and I know will take me a lifetime to master: Living Directionally. I will end this book with this concept, and I look forward to getting into it more deeply in the next one.

For now, the basic idea is to live your life with a focus on always creating how you want to live and where you want to go. To address this concept in a clear way, I'll break it down into four principles:

1 Mindset
2 Discipline
3 Goals
4 Accountability

Let's start with mindset. This is my direction on how you can approach things in the healthiest way: by staying positive and letting yourself be open to gratitude. Instead of thinking you'll never get what you want in life, start looking for all the positive things you already have—no matter how small—and be grateful for them. Once you train yourself to recognize those bits of goodness, you'll be well on your way to setting your mindset in a direction that sees the possibilities in life—not the failures.

Discipline is what my husband would call my defining characteristic—through all the ups and downs in my life, discipline is what has always kept me grounded. I guarantee if you cultivate discipline in your life, you won't regret the work. Discipline is the quality that you will want to push forward, even when things are tough or a roadblock gets in your way. As I've said throughout this book, there are really only two ways to go in this life: toward your goals or away from them. Discipline will keep you faced in a consistent direction.

To get anywhere it's a good idea to know where you are going. And that's where goals come in. Your goal might be to ultimately manage the department you are in at work. Or if you tend to spend too many hours at the office, your goal might be to spend at least two hours with your family every night after you get home. Maybe you're a super introvert and your goal is to reach out and build a bigger community of friends. Whatever it is, define it and write it down.

Finally, hold yourself accountable for what you want. None of the other steps will work if you don't commit to each one and actually take ownership. And it's okay if one night you worked until midnight and didn't spend time with your family. Accept that as a speed bump and keep striving toward your goal. Our lives are never going to be perfect. Remember, progress over perfection. They can be better and happier, and you don't need to spend time beating yourself up over failures.

When we combine movement with intentional choices and clear vision, good things happen. That is the heart of living directionally.

Each one of us only has so much energy to expend at any given time, so we have to decide strategically where to place it. I call this my rule of energy allocation. Throughout the day, we are constantly

deciding where our energy goes . . . and one thing is clear: When we try to spread it too thin, nothing really gets done. Think about your goals and make sure your energy is focused on them. For example, this book has received a great deal of my energy as I've been writing it. Because of that, I've been doing less coaching. Where we put our energy is where positive growth occurs. Choose deliberately and reallocate as necessary. Moving toward your goals should make you more energized and emotionally stronger.

Movement is our most tangible proof of energy: We really know what's happening when we get physical. Energy can also be intangible: emotional, intellectual, or spiritual. Those are a bit more abstract. When we give energy to something physical, we feel it in a direct way—we're tired or we feel stronger. It's easy to get behind it and engage with it. Movement is motivation. For my coaching clients, I offer movement meetings where we do a physical activity, indoors or out. We physically move toward something positive, together. We experience, in a very

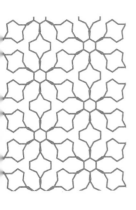

Where we put our energy is where positive growth occurs. Choose deliberately and reallocate as necessary.

tangible way, what it means to live directionally. Feeling that physical movement can help you with the intangible efforts of living directionally. As you get closer to your goals you will feel better, clearer, and emotionally and psychologically stronger.

After I lost my brother, I spent much of middle and high school trying to fill the hole in my heart left by his passing. At the same time, in a way I can only understand now, losing Michael is also what gave my life purpose. That loss and his life are why I take all life—mine and yours—so seriously: I appreciate that we get just one shot at this and "I am not throwing away my shot" (as the *Hamilton* song goes). And I'm not going to let you throw away yours.

When we look at the lives of others, particularly those who are very successful, it's natural to wonder how they achieved that level of success—especially if we happen to be going through a hard time. How did they manage to have the fantastic career, the happy marriage, the large and loving family, the fill-in-the-blank fabulous thing that I don't have? Instead of obsessing over what they have and what you don't, let their success inspire you to follow through on your own vision. When we look at super-successful people, we start to notice certain patterns. I'll bet if you look more closely at what they did to achieve success, you'll see that they followed their own vision and goals and set themselves on a course, making positive, intentional decisions along the way. It's not easy for anyone. Success is something you make for yourself, strategically, systematically, and creatively.

When you live directionally, each day is an opportunity to move yourself toward your Best Version (page 20). Doing this can be challenging. Negativity creeps in, and we have to do what we can to push it out. When that happens, focus on your plan, and you will defuse any creeping negative energy. Steer toward the things you want, the things that make you happy, and make you feel good. Being happy and healthy requires vigilance and work, and the more you practice that, the more natural it will become. Notice I didn't say easier: This work is never easy. It's hard. But anything worth having is not going to be easy. It does become more natural, a part of your everyday life. And you have the tools and support you need to make it happen.

The one tool I'd like to emphasize when living directionally is Think It, Write It, Share It (see page 20). Once I have my goal and my plan, I make sure to write it down, and then I gather up all my courage and I share it. Maybe I'll tell my husband or a friend. Sometimes I really go for it and share it on Facebook, Instagram, or Twitter. When I share my goals and plans, they become real—and I have committed in public to making them happen. I encourage you to do the same.

A picture really is worth a thousand words, although sometimes, we can't put our finger on exactly what it is we want. Even if we can't always put it into words, we can envision a general direction—and if you head in that direction, the picture will become clearer. You'll know when you've found what you've been looking for because you'll feel it with an uplifting sense of triumph. Although you may not be able to describe the house you want to call home, the perfect job and work place, you will recognize all that when you see it. When you're living directionally, you will be actively making decisions toward that image, that vision. So, in this final Life Lesson, I ask you to use the power of your mind to formulate a picture of your life as you want to live it. Living directionally is living toward that picture, and in doing so you'll increase the possibility of eventually making it real.

It can be hard to visualize having something you haven't had before. As you explore taking care of these parts of life for yourself, check in with your support systems and ask for help. This book came to be because I shared my intention to author it. I could have procrastinated

DON'T LET CHALLENGES
GET THE BETTER OF YOU—
GET IN THE HABIT OF
CHALLENGING THEM BACK.

over this project by dwelling on how dyslexia always made reading and writing a challenge for me. That would've been easy! Instead, I chose to do something harder: I actively looked for a cowriter, and when I found one, together we motivated each other until we made this book happen.

We all need help. Just because I am a life coach doesn't mean I don't need help myself. Quite the opposite: I am all about giving and receiving help. I'm proud to say that I've always been really good at knowing exactly where to go whenever I've needed help, and I've never been shy about asking; my struggles lie elsewhere. If you take away just one thing from this book, I hope it's this: Let these Life Lessons empower you to ask for help whenever and wherever you need it. Don't let challenges get the better of you—get in the habit of challenging them back.

We all need someone to talk to, someone to listen. I could never have arrived at this moment of peace in my own life had I not collaborated with many, many amazing

THINKWORK

- When you shut your eyes and imagine a big, beautiful picture of your life, what do you see?
- Describe it in as much detail as possible. Then write it down.
- Name three ways you plan to begin moving toward this vision.

WHAT'S YOUR NEXT STEP?

This is the question I ask at the close of every coaching session, every speaking engagement, every family meeting. After absorbing the eleven lessons here, you have all the tools you need to get out there, define your goals, and move yourself toward them. You will absolutely run into speed bumps, other drivers that will slow you down, and passengers will try to distract you. That's okay, because that's life. All you want to remember is to keep your eye on your goal and know that you can go back to any lesson any time and recharge your resolve. Sometimes life gets tough; I hope these eleven lessons can always be part of your support. They are here to help. So ask yourself my signature question: What's my next step? Look at your calendar or iPhone, decide on a date, and create an invite to start mapping out your most inspired goal. Why is this so important? Because putting a date on it makes it real. If you don't have a next step, you're going nowhere. It's that simple. And I am all about movement: positive direction toward your Best Version.

people. Whether or not you have someone to share with privately right now, I hope this book helps. I hope you'll use it as a confidant, something you keep close to you and open to any page for instant motivation, or just a friendly reminder. Fill the book with notes (every book I own is marked up everywhere). Wherever you find a spot that resonates, highlight it and when you ready, share what you've written. And most of all, live your vision: Live directionally.

ACKNOWLEGMENTS

All books are collaborations—one of the many reasons I enjoyed this project so much. This book would have never happened without the following people (I'm still kind of pinching myself that it has!):

I am especially grateful to my publisher, Angela Engel, and her team at the Collective Book Studio: You listened to my message and ran with it. Amy Treadwell, thank you! I loved sharing these Life Lessons with you and enjoyed every one of our writing and editing sessions. To Julia Szabo, thanks for helping me find my voice and for getting my ideas on paper! Seeing my philosophy made into a manuscript was a lifelong goal achieved—you helped make this project a possibility. Simply no way to thank you enough.

Thanks to all the stylists who helped make this book beautiful: My home stylist AJ Cafutto, Michael Giannelli at East Hampton Gardens, makeup artists Amber D'Angelo Chi Chi Saito, and Victoria Schade. Hair cover shot and Hamptons hair by Braydon Nelson and my go-to girl Racquel Benedetto Peterson. I always feel my most beautiful, inside and out, with all of you by my side.

Thank you to Georgia Louise, my esthetician, and Andrea Curry, my yoga teacher, for my glow as we prepped for photo shoots. I'm lucky to have you both.

Liza Gershman, thank you for the stunning photography in NYC. We did our best to shoot what we could while the city was shutting down around us in mid-March. We had no idea what COVID-19 had in store for all of us for the rest of the year. And thank you to Madison Fender who stepped up in a pinch and came to the rescue with her camera and snapped our cover.

To my Hill Country family: Thank you for the hospitality and inspiration. Often our first stop on a Thursday date night, you are our home away from home.

To my wonderful Mom and Dad and my incredibly supportive in-laws, MomG and DadG: Thank you for continuing to love and support me. And to my sister, Tara: Thank you for helping me laugh—mostly at myself.

Lastly, to my high school friends and my communities, both in Manhattan and the East End: Home is everything to me, so thank you for being my family's safe harbor. I am so incredibly grateful to you all!

IN LOVING MEMORY OF MY
BROTHER, MICHAEL JON.
I MISS YOU AND THINK
ABOUT YOU EVERY DAY.
AND I'LL HOLD YOU IN MY
HEART ALWAYS.

HAPPINESS IS A SERIES OF GOOD DECISIONS · LIVE DIRECTIONALLY · IT'S ONLY A PROBLEM IF YOU MAKE IT A PROBLEM · DO WHAT WORKS · TRADITIONS: HONOR THEM, CREATE THEM, KEEP THEM · IF IT'S NOT RIGHT, GO LEFT · LOVE IS A CHOICE · STAY IN YOUR LANE · STOP WINE-ING · BEGIN. FOCUS. COMMIT. · CHANGE IS HARD AND CHANGE IS GOOD

EM · IF IT'S NOT RIGHT, GO LEFT · LOVE IS A CHOICE · STAY IN YOUR LANE · STOP WINE
YOU MAKE IT A PROBLEM · BEGIN. FOCUS. COMMIT. · CHANGE IS HARD AND CHANGE IS
GHT, GO LEFT · LOVE IS A CHOICE · STAY IN YOUR LANE · STOP WINE-ING · HAPPINESS
PROBLEM · BEGIN. FOCUS. COMMIT. · CHANGE IS HARD AND CHANGE IS GOOD · DO WHAT
VE IS A CHOICE · STAY IN YOUR LANE · STOP WINE-ING · HAPPINESS IS A SERIES OF GOO
CUS. COMMIT. · CHANGE IS HARD AND CHANGE IS GOOD · DO WHAT WORKS · TRADITION
AY IN YOUR LANE · STOP WINE-ING · HAPPINESS IS A SERIES OF GOOD DECISIONS · LIVE
ANGE IS HARD AND CHANGE IS GOOD · DO WHAT WORKS · TRADITIONS: HONOR THEM. CR
TOP WINE-ING · HAPPINESS IS A SERIES OF GOOD DECISIONS · LIVE DIRECTIONALLY · IT
ANGE IS GOOD · DO WHAT WORKS · TRADITIONS: HONOR THEM. CREATE THEM. KEEP TH
PPINESS IS A SERIES OF GOOD DECISIONS · LIVE DIRECTIONALLY · IT'S ONLY A PROBLE
O WHAT WORKS · TRADITIONS: HONOR THEM. CREATE THEM. KEEP THEM · IF IT'S NOT RIG
GOOD DECISIONS · LIVE DIRECTIONALLY · IT'S ONLY A PROBLEM IF YOU MAKE IT A P
ADITIONS: HONOR THEM. CREATE THEM. KEEP THEM · IF IT'S NOT RIGHT, GO LEFT · LOVE
IVE DIRECTIONALLY · IT'S ONLY A PROBLEM IF YOU MAKE IT A PROBLEM · BEGIN. FOCUS.
EATE THEM. KEEP THEM · IF IT'S NOT RIGHT, GO LEFT · LOVE IS A CHOICE · STAY IN YO
T'S ONLY A PROBLEM IF YOU MAKE IT A PROBLEM · BEGIN. FOCUS. COMMIT. · CHANGE IS
EM · IF IT'S NOT RIGHT, GO LEFT · LOVE IS A CHOICE · STAY IN YOUR LANE · STOP WINE
YOU MAKE IT A PROBLEM · BEGIN. FOCUS. COMMIT. · CHANGE IS HARD AND CHANGE IS
GHT, GO LEFT · LOVE IS A CHOICE · STAY IN YOUR LANE · STOP WINE-ING · HAPPINESS
PROBLEM · BEGIN. FOCUS. COMMIT. · CHANGE IS HARD AND CHANGE IS GOOD · DO WHAT
VE IS A CHOICE · STAY IN YOUR LANE · STOP WINE-ING · HAPPINESS IS A SERIES OF GOO
CUS. COMMIT. · CHANGE IS HARD AND CHANGE IS GOOD · DO WHAT WORKS · TRADITION
AY IN YOUR LANE · STOP WINE-ING · HAPPINESS IS A SERIES OF GOOD DECISIONS · LIVE
ANGE IS HARD AND CHANGE IS GOOD · DO WHAT WORKS · TRADITIONS: HONOR THEM. CR
TOP WINE-ING · HAPPINESS IS A SERIES OF GOOD DECISIONS · LIVE DIRECTIONALLY · IT
ANGE IS GOOD · DO WHAT WORKS · TRADITIONS: HONOR THEM. CREATE THEM. KEEP TH
PPINESS IS A SERIES OF GOOD DECISIONS · LIVE DIRECTIONALLY · IT'S ONLY A PROBLE
O WHAT WORKS · TRADITIONS: HONOR THEM. CREATE THEM. KEEP THEM · IF IT'S NOT RIG
GOOD DECISIONS · LIVE DIRECTIONALLY · IT'S ONLY A PROBLEM IF YOU MAKE IT A P
ADITIONS: HONOR THEM. CREATE THEM. KEEP THEM · IF IT'S NOT RIGHT, GO LEFT · LOVE
IVE DIRECTIONALLY · IT'S ONLY A PROBLEM IF YOU MAKE IT A PROBLEM · BEGIN. FOCUS.
EATE THEM. KEEP THEM · IF IT'S NOT RIGHT, GO LEFT · LOVE IS A CHOICE · STAY IN YO
T'S ONLY A PROBLEM IF YOU MAKE IT A PROBLEM · BEGIN. FOCUS. COMMIT. · CHANGE IS
EM · IF IT'S NOT RIGHT, GO LEFT · LOVE IS A CHOICE · STAY IN YOUR LANE · STOP WINE
YOU MAKE IT A PROBLEM · BEGIN. FOCUS. COMMIT. · CHANGE IS HARD AND CHANGE IS
GHT, GO LEFT · LOVE IS A CHOICE · STAY IN YOUR LANE · STOP WINE-ING · HAPPINESS
PROBLEM · BEGIN. FOCUS. COMMIT. · CHANGE IS HARD AND CHANGE IS GOOD · DO WHAT
VE IS A CHOICE · STAY IN YOUR LANE · STOP WINE-ING · HAPPINESS IS A SERIES OF GOO
CUS. COMMIT. · CHANGE IS HARD AND CHANGE IS GOOD · DO WHAT WORKS · TRADITION
AY IN YOUR LANE · STOP WINE-ING · HAPPINESS IS A SERIES OF GOOD DECISIONS · LIVE
ANGE IS HARD AND CHANGE IS GOOD · DO WHAT WORKS · TRADITIONS: HONOR THEM. CR
TOP WINE-ING · HAPPINESS IS A SERIES OF GOOD DECISIONS · LIVE DIRECTIONALLY · IT
ANGE IS GOOD · DO WHAT WORKS · TRADITIONS: HONOR THEM. CREATE THEM. KEEP TH
PPINESS IS A SERIES OF GOOD DECISIONS · LIVE DIRECTIONALLY · IT'S ONLY A PROBLE
O WHAT WORKS · TRADITIONS: HONOR THEM. CREATE THEM. KEEP THEM · IF IT'S NOT RIG
GOOD DECISIONS · LIVE DIRECTIONALLY · IT'S ONLY A PROBLEM IF YOU MAKE IT A P
ADITIONS: HONOR THEM. CREATE THEM. KEEP THEM · IF IT'S NOT RIGHT, GO LEFT · LOVE
IVE DIRECTIONALLY · IT'S ONLY A PROBLEM IF YOU MAKE IT A PROBLEM · BEGIN. FOCUS.
EATE THEM. KEEP THEM · IF IT'S NOT RIGHT, GO LEFT · LOVE IS A CHOICE · STAY IN YO